STOP SCROLLING

30 DAYS TO HEALTHY SCREEN TIME HABITS (WITHOUT THROWING YOUR PHONE AWAY)

TONY WRIGHTON

LEGAL BIT

The information in this book has been provided for informational, educational and entertainment purposes only. It is not designed to replace or take the place of any form of therapy or professional medical advice. The information contained in this book has been compiled from sources deemed reliable, and it is accurate to the best of the Author's knowledge; however, the Author cannot guarantee its accuracy and validity and cannot be held liable for any errors or omissions. Upon using the information contained in this book, you agree to hold harmless the Author, and Publisher, from and against any damages, costs, and expenses, including any legal fees potentially resulting from the application of any of the information provided by this guide. This disclaimer applies to any damages or injury caused by the use and application, whether directly or indirectly, of any advice or information presented, whether for breach of contract, tort, negligence, personal injury, criminal intent, or under any other cause of action. You agree to accept all risks of using the information presented inside this book. And whatever happens, definitely don't throw your phone away. Legal bit over. Copyright © 2022 Tony Wrighton

ABOUT THE AUTHOR

Tony Wrighton is a UK-based journalist and broadcaster. His books have been translated into 12 languages, including Spanish, Italian, Japanese, Chinese, Turkish, Dutch and Croatian.

His broadcasting career has spanned two decades, being a regular presenter on channels including Sky News, Sky Sports News, ITV and LBC. He also hosts a podcast called *Zestology*.

OTHER 30 DAY TITLES

Learn NLP: Master Neuro-Linguistic Programming (the Non-Boring Way) in 30 Days

CONTENTS

What To Expect 9

Introduction 11

Day 1 – Small Changes, Big Results..............................17

Day 2 – Recharging...20

Day 3 – Connected Devices 23

Day 4 – Bed-Scrolling...26

Day 5 – Virtual Decluttering..29

Day 6 – Measuring Things..34

Day 7 – Lock Up Your Cookies......................................38

Day 8 – Alone For The Night 43

Day 9 – Optimal Morning Routine 46

Day 10 – Vision Breaks 49

Day 11 – Scroll Apnea 53

Day 12 – Taste The Raisin 56

Day 13 – Gray Matter...59

Day 14 – The Setback Effect...61

Day 15 – Slap Screen...64

Day 16 – Sharing Is Caring 67

Day 17 – Movement Snacks..71

Day 18 – Creative Quietude 75

Day 19 – Be More Jobs 78

Day 20 – Micro Reminders 81

Day 21 – Screen Time to Green Time 86

Day 22 – Blocking Sites 91

Day 23 – Are You An E-voider? 93

Day 24 – Supplements 97

Day 25 – Logical Levels 101

Day 26 – Task Batching 104

Day 27 – Alter Your Brainwaves 107

Day 28 – Upgrade or Downgrade? 111

Day 29 – Nuance 114

Day 30 – 1170 Reasons To Celebrate 117

Day 31 Onwards – Regular Refreshers 121

Take another *30 Day Expert* program 122

References 125

WHAT TO EXPECT

> *"Man who invented the mobile phone says people need to 'get a life'."*
>
> *– Metro Newspaper Headline, 30th June 2022.*

This book is for you if:

- You wake up and scroll before breakfast.
- You take your phone to the toilet (yes, you).
- You tap your dead phone for alerts.
- You feel on edge when you can't check your messages.
- You feel stressed, anxious, and busy, or you have a backlog of 18 messages waiting for a reply.
- You want to get more focused, creative, productive and happy.
- You are currently scrolling on your device for the 194th time today

The science around scrolling is piling up. Too much screen time is bad for our physical and mental health. It is linked to an alarming cocktail of anxiety, depression, and poor diet, health and sleep (1, 2, 3). We now spend an average of almost six hours a day (yes, six) on email (4). Young US TikTok users average 87 minutes a day on that site alone. (5). We are literally scrolling away our lives.

So over the next 30 days, you'll learn to

1. **Scroll a bit less.**
2. **Scroll a bit smarter.**

Each day is a mini-chapter containing a proven screen time change you can use straight away. And don't worry; you don't have to throw your phone away. We're just going to scroll a bit smarter, using NLP techniques and the latest in behavioral science. It's really pretty painless.

We're going to change our unhealthy screen habits, starting now. In the words of the man who invented the mobile phone, it's time to "get a life".

INTRODUCTION

Hi, I'm Tony, and I'm addicted to scrolling. Or at least I was. I'm getting over it now, with the help of the techniques in this book. Here's a little more about me.

- I'm a journalist and wellness author. My books have been translated into 12 languages.
- I started writing about wellness and personal development two decades ago. Yes, pre-Facebook.
- I work hard at healthy online behavior. Yet I am still addicted to the tiny pleasures of a tweet, ping or like.
- Fun fact: pre-scroll addiction, my friend and I actually shared an email address when we went traveling in Asia. Yes, that's how innocent life was.

I've always had issues with focus and attention span. My science teacher once said in a school report that I was "bone idle". I may have been mischievous, but this was unfair. I love learning and working; I'm just easily distracted. I have to work really hard at focusing (so scrolling is my kryptonite).

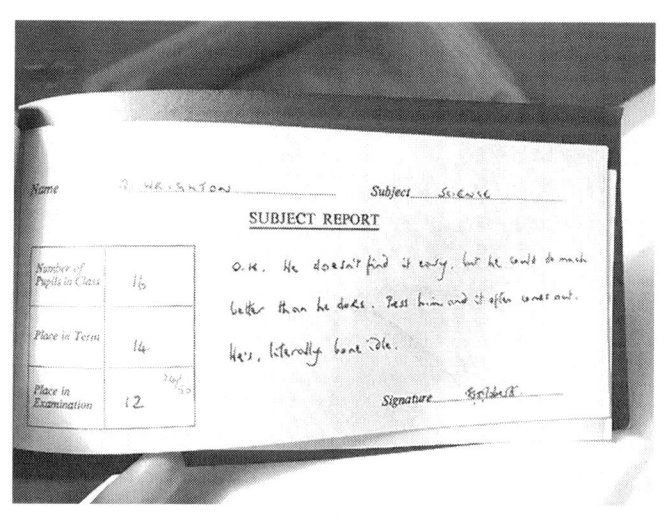

"He's, literally bone idle." *A very unfair school report. Perhaps my teacher should have focused more on his own poor grammar.*

This problem of distraction now seems to be affecting everyone, even people who didn't come near the bottom of the class at school because they couldn't focus. And it's because of screens. The number of hours per week we spend pixel-gazing is off the charts, but we just can't stop.

Over the course of this program, I will lay out some of the incredible science that shows just how distracting our screen time has become. And then we will reduce those distractions. We will stop, press pause and recharge.

This problem of distraction is not a new one

Frédéric Chopin was one of the world's most celebrated composers. He lived in Paris in the 19th century, and was an urban creature. He enjoyed living in the city and all of the distractions that life there had to offer. Obviously, this was 200 years ago and those distractions did not include a regularly refreshed TikTok feed. But there was still plenty for Chopin to amuse himself with in Paris.

Every summer he would escape the city and go to his partner's house in the country. Novelist Aurore Dupin (known by her pen name George Sand) had a retreat in the French countryside. Chopin found the pace of rural life painfully slow, but this was where his creativity became supercharged. The quieter pace meant fewer distractions, and he would write music more productively than he could ever do in the city.

Sand described the way that Chopin would wake early, have a simple breakfast and then spend the entire day composing, because *there was nothing else to do*. He would absorb himself for, as she described it, weeks at a time, on a single page of musical note-taking. After six weeks, he would often abandon all of his scribblings and go back to the original composition, which had been just right.

The more Chopin eliminated his day-to-day diversions, the more he was able to create his finest work. Truthfully, it wasn't all idyllic. Apparently he would sometimes sulk in his room and break his pens in frustration. Yet, this was all part of the creative process. His genius could only truly express itself without distraction and interruption.

Let's be honest, he was lucky he didn't have instagram. Or a phone. Or a laptop. Or unlimited wifi. And despite having none of that, he *still* needed to escape the city to get his work done. This suggests this problem of distraction is not a new one.

Fast forward to today though, and all of our brains are overworked. Screens are now taking information overload to a level significantly more problematic than in Chopin's day. His sort of single-minded creativity and brilliance is becoming a rarity. Chopin was a world-renowned musician, and, to be at his best, he had to reduce the amount of information coming in. As Nicholas Carr observes in his excellent book *The Shallows: What the Internet is Doing to Our Brains;*

"When our brain is overtaxed, we find distractions more distracting."

We will explore this idea of *distracting distractions* in depth over the next 30 days. We will reduce our reliance on screens, and indulge in some healthy scrolling. And it won't involve locking yourself in your room and breaking your pens. You will feel happier, healthier, more motivated and more inspired, and you'll have a lot more time on your hands too.

How this *30 Day Expert* program works

> *"It is a paradox that by emptying our lives of distractions we are actually filling the well."*
> – Julia Cameron.

You'll be following small daily prompts over the course of 30 days. Each day has been put together using the latest in science and research to ensure you actually complete the program and successfully wean yourself off the infinite scroll. You'll be "filling the well".

As mentioned previously, we will have lazer-like focus on:

1. Scrolling a bit less.
2. Scrolling a bit smarter.

I use the words "a bit" deliberately. This is not a hardcore approach to screen time. You don't have to lock your phone in a cupboard, and we won't be confiscating your devices for the next month. The skills of Neuro-Linguistic Programming (NLP) are perfectly tailored to ensuring you start controlling your tech usage, rather than letting the tech control you.

About NLP

NLP is a set of skills and theories (with a rather long title) that were first developed in the 1970s. I started studying it almost 20 years ago. It's a powerful set of techniques focusing on how people communicate with themselves and others. We can use NLP to "rewire" our inner thought processes, and ensure the changes we make are for keeps.

Over the years, I have progressed through the levels of Practitioner, Master Practitioner and Trainer and written books on

NLP that have been published across the world. More recently, I discovered something exciting. It turns out these skills work particularly well when applied to healthier screen time.

In this program, I combine these NLP techniques with the world's best behavioral science and research. I include references so you can go and see for yourself why these techniques work so well in helping you escape the screens, focus better, think clearer and create extra time in your day.

Remember, nobody's saying you have to quit scrolling forever. Tech will start to work for you, rather than against you.

Keeping an open mind

A key NLP principle that has helped millions of people is "The Law of Requisite Variety". Here's how it works:

"The more variety you can introduce into your life, the more you can adjust and operate at your best."

This is a law well worth respecting during this *30 Day Expert* program. It means you should be as open-minded and flexible as possible. It tells us that, when we're doing something that isn't working, we should try something else. That's why there is a rich selection of methods for healthier screen time in this book. The key is to embrace the techniques with an open mind and see what works.

Not all of them will resonate with you, but The Law of Requisite Variety says that, the more you sample different techniques, the more effectively you can figure out a healthy personal tech use strategy. Basically, this is my way of saying, "Don't just discard something because it sounds weird. Give it a go first.".

As a brief example, on Day 5 we investigate a whole host of methods and apps for 'virtual decluttering'. My personal favorite is *ScreenZen*; that's my go-to on a daily basis. But yours might be different. After sampling them all, you may prefer *Later* or *Forest* or another one.

So here's how to read this book:

1. Follow the daily prompts and tick off the To Do List at the end of the day.
2. Try everything and see what resonates best with you. The Law of Requisite Variety says this makes lasting changes more likely.
3. You end up with your own unique template for operating at your best around screens.

DAY 1

Small Changes, Big Results

> *"Hey Weekly Screen Time report, I'm not proud of it either."*
> *– Field Yates, Twitter*

Excessive screen time is bad for our physical and mental health. The studies are snowballing. They show links between heavy screen use and an increased risk of anxiety (1), depression (2), poor diet, health and sleep (3), and more. This is a serious problem, and one that is getting worse.

So, in Week 1, we're going to employ a simple strategy to scroll for a few minutes less a day. That's it.

You will be reading, watching and scrolling (a bit) less, and creating more time in which to get stuff done. The cumulative effect of doing this over 30 days will be powerful. Consider this from author Josh Waitzkin.

> *"When nothing exciting is going on, we might get bored, distracted, separated from the moment. So we look for new entertainment, surf channels, flip through magazines. If caught in these rhythms, we are like tiny current-bound surface fish, floating along in a two-dimensional world without any sense for the gorgeous abyss below."*
> *– Josh Waitzkin, The Art Of Learning*

Today, we allow ourselves to explore Waitzkin's "gorgeous abyss below".

Start small at first

Scroller Steve starts Day 1 enthusiastically. He decides to go all in and quit screens for four hours a day. But a problem arises. He's out with his friends and hasn't brought his wallet. He wants to buy drinks, so he briefly opens up his phone and uses Apple Pay. Multiple notifications pop up, and, obviously, he checks them. Later, another problem emerges. Scroller Steve needs to call an Uber. But for that, he'll have to turn on his screen again. Oh, dear. Scroller Steve soon gives up on his good intentions. It's just too hard to live without a phone all day long. And besides, he's got 17 messages to reply to.

In my two decades of working in behavioral change and NLP, I have found one simple factor that seems to have the biggest impact on changing habits; don't be too ambitious when you start out with a new behavior.

The concept was popularized by James Clear in his book *Atomic Habits: An Easy & Proven Way to Build Good Habits & Break Bad Ones*.

Clear found that one of the reasons we don't stick with New Year's resolutions, new goals and new outcomes is that we're too enthusiastic. We aim too high. The science backs this up. The University of Scranton found that almost half of all Americans set New Year's Resolutions every year, and a whopping 92% of them fail. That means 132 million Americans fail at goal-setting each year (4).

So here (and indeed all my *30 Day Expert* programs) we are going to start very small, and then gradually increase our efforts as we go.

Starting with the basics

I know, you are probably ready to go all in. You may want to go cold turkey. You might intend to turn your house into a calm oasis. You could even be planning to dump all your screens in the nearest skip. But hold on. I want to ensure that you complete the 30 days. We are looking for changes that last, so that you start to form a healthier relationship with the screens around you.

What we repeat becomes a habit over time. So for the first week, we start with the bar low. We are looking to reduce our scrolling and the amount of information coming in for a tiny sliver of your day.

> Today, your *Stop Scrolling* program involves putting all your screens for just 15 scroll-free minutes. I know 15 minutes doesn't seem long. You're welcome to do more than 15 minutes if you'd like. Just as long as you do the first 15, you're good.

It may not feel like you are doing much today, but throughout this program, we allow ourselves to be guided by well-established habit-forming principles. Dr. BJ Fogg leads the Persuasive Technology Lab at Stanford University. He says, "when you start small, your ability to do the habit is very high regardless of your motivation."

So we are going for small, easy changes that last.

TO-DO LIST

- ☐ **Switch off for 15 minutes and briefly embrace a "Low Information Diet".**
- ☐ **That's it. We start by making small changes, as per the science.**

DAY 2

Recharging

> *"I wonder how many miles I've scrolled on my phone."*
> *– Shower Thoughts on Twitter*

Cal Newport is a celebrated author on the subject of productivity and deep work. I have three of his books at home and they've helped me quit doomscrolling, zombie scrolling, and other scrolling sub-genres. So I reached out to him, and we set up an interview. I asked him on my podcast *Zestology* what all this screen use is doing to our brain.

He told me that our devices are affecting the way our Paleolithic brains work. Some workers have been observed to check their email more than 400 times a day, and on average, three working hours per day are being lost to scrolling: emails, social media and so on. These are valuable hours that could be spent achieving a better work-life balance.

It became clear that what I needed was something to focus on instead of scrolling. From a behavioral perspective, I required something different to think about. Here's a little game to show why.

Don't think of a pink tiger

What did you think of? Almost certainly, a pink tiger.

Admittedly, that probably wasn't the best game you've ever played, but hopefully it demonstrated the command I gave you was not helpful. At some level, your brain has to think of a pink tiger in order to not think of a pink tiger.

One of the many reasons people find it so hard to become a "non-smoker" is that their brain has to register the word "smoker" whenever the word is said. So in our journey to mastering our scrolling, we need to give ourselves a strong, positive behavioral command.

> ➢ Think of the precious moments you spend away from screens as "recharging".

We don't focus specifically on "stopping scrolling" or reducing our screen time (even though that's our aim) because we want to express our goal in a way that doesn't use the words "scrolling" or "screen time". It's recharging…

- Recharging your energy levels
- Recharging your mind, attention span and focus
- Recharging your own body battery

Your recharging time focuses on the things that you love. After all, most of the best things in life don't involve scrolling. Right? Fun, food, friendship, other things beginning with F… you get the picture.

Cal Newport is all about getting deep work done in a connected age. And he summed up really well why we need this time to recharge.

"We fear solitude, but it's exactly this time alone with our own thoughts that we need to make sense of our experiences and grow as humans. TikTok is fun, but grappling with the core questions of our existence is fundamental."

Stop Scrolling

TO-DO LIST

- ☐ **Switch off for 15 minutes.**
- ☐ **Focus on *recharging***

DAY 3

Connected Devices

"Airpods in. Volume up. Ignore the world."

– Unknown

There are some non-scrollable devices that still count in our Stop Scrolling program. So don't think you can get away with AirPods. Sure, you can't scroll on them, but you can google stuff, talk to Siri and send emails. Basically, you can cheat. (And trust me, I've done plenty of that on my scrolling journey.)

It's not just the AirPods. Today, we need to have a tough conversation about some "scroll extras". These are devices that aren't technically scrollable but can have the same effect. For the avoidance of doubt, when we are switched off and in recharging mode, the following devices are banned:

- AirPods
- Google Home
- Alexa
- Connected Speakers
- Connected Glasses
- Fitbits
- Any fitness trackers
- Apple Watches
- Whoop Bands
- Virtual Reality Headsets

If you are struggling to figure out if something should be switched off while you are recharging, you can ask these questions:

- ➢ Does it connect to the internet?
- ➢ Is it something our ancestors would have used?

Clearly, our ancestors wouldn't have listened to a podcast on wireless earbuds, but they would have enjoyed cooking, sunbathing, walking, running or even talking to friends.

"Alexa, Are You Invading My Privacy?"

Devices like Alexa are always on even when they're 'not listening', as they need to be ready to respond to their wake word. Technology is often wonderful, but I don't want to be surrounded by connected devices in my house.

You may not want to go as all-in as me, but I have set up my life and home to be as unconnected as possible. That means no Alexa, no Phillips Hue lighting and no internet-connected robot vacuum cleaners. Even my air purifier wants to connect to Wi-Fi – er, no thanks. I do use a wearable fitness tracker (Oura Ring) but it doesn't have a screen and has a built-in airplane mode.

All of this helps with distraction, EMF exposure and privacy. Admittedly, I do have to get up to dim the lights myself.

There is a potential double win linked to switching devices off. I chatted to award-winning tech journalist August Brice about how some people display a particular sensitivity to the EMFs (Electro-Magnetic Fields) that our devices give off. She has researched the subject extensively, and says this type of very low-level radiation has been proven to have biological effects.

She's noticed symptoms such as anxiety, headaches, palpitations, tinnitus, ringing in the ears, brain fog and dizziness being linked to Electro-Magnetic Fields. As far as devices are concerned, she told me the EMF comparison between AirPods and normal wired headphones is particularly interesting. You can listen to *Zestology* episode #380 for more on this or Google "air-tube headsets" for a low-EMF listening experience.

It should be noted that the subject of EMFs and health is controversial. Not everyone agrees they are worth worrying about. But the World Health Organisation classified mobile phone radiation as a "possible" human carcinogen in 2011, and the governments of the United Kingdom, France and Israel have issued warnings against mobile phone use by children (1).

TO-DO LIST

- ☐ **Switch off for 15 minutes. Recharge.**
- ☐ **Switch off connected tech (eg. AirPods, Alexa) during your recharging time.**

DAY 4

Bed-Scrolling

> *"The phone is the anti-sleep device."*
> *– Adam McKay, film director and host of Bedtime Stories with Adam McKay*

It's now true that, for most people, the last thing we look at before we fall asleep is a tiny illuminated device in the dark. Normally it's about two inches from our faces. It means scrolling and screens spill over into every area of our lives. And come on, let's be honest with ourselves – we all sort of instinctively know that staring goggle-eyed at screens in bed is not a particularly healthy thing to do.

Our circadian rhythm (the body's internal 24-hour clock) is being badly affected by bed-scrolling. The phone is the anti-sleep device, and I have a favorite study that perfectly demonstrates this.

Scientists at the University of Colorado Boulder sent a number of participants camping in the Rocky Mountains. They left all their screens behind. No phones, laptops or other devices were present. In fact, they weren't even allowed a flashlight.

After a few days, researchers found the campers started sleeping longer. They were getting a lovely 10 hours sleep on average, as opposed to the usual seven and a half.

Why was this? The campers were being exposed to up to 13 times more natural light than they would have been at home, and no artificial light. Tuning in with nature and cutting out artificial light meant they were sleeping longer and more deeply (1).

In a few days, we're going to be banning bed-scrolling. No more screens in bed. It'll help your sleep, and it'll help improve your morning as well.

This is a big step for many people, so we will take a few days to prepare for it. The most common reasons people fail to leave their screens out of the bedroom are that:

1. They use their phone as an alarm clock.
2. They use their phone as a flashlight.

These are obviously entirely valid reasons. But once the phone sneaks into the bedroom – guess what – we're online at 3am mindlessly scrolling through emails from HR or cat videos.

So, today you have two tasks:

- If you use your phone as an alarm clock: get an alarm clock. This is a small investment that will pay itself back many times over. You can get one second-hand virtually free on eBay, Facebook Marketplace or Vinted.
- You also need to get a piece of red light gel filter (normally under $8 on Amazon or cheaper second-hand). You will need to cut this sheet of red plastic into the shape of your alarm clock and put it over the display. This ensures the light of the clock does not affect your circadian rhythm.
- If you use your phone as a flashlight: buy a small, cheap one. Again, second-hand will do. Put the red light gel over the flashlight.

I want to make this program as cost-effective and easy as possible. There is no excuse for having the phone in the bedroom once you have something else that will tell you the time in your room.

There is one more way I like to set up my no-screen bedroom. I keep a small pad and pen by my bed. This is because, once I quit bed-scrolling, I found I was having my best ideas just before I went to sleep, first thing in the morning and even in the middle of the night. And I would forget them if I didn't write them down.

TO-DO LIST

- ☐ **Switch off for 15 minutes. Recharge.**
- ☐ **Get cheap alarm clock + torch in place. Prepare your no-screen bedroom.**

DAY 5

Virtual Decluttering

> *"My mind is like my web browser: 19 tabs are open, 3 of them are frozen, and I have no idea where the music is coming from."*
>
> – Anonymous

The celebrated Brazilian author Paulo Coelho owns a huge apartment in Geneva, Switzerland. If you walked in, you would see almost nothing at all. He keeps his impressive home almost entirely empty.

Coelho understands the importance of minimal clutter. He says, "empty space is my biggest indulgence." He understands the simplicity and the pleasure of a tidy, focused and aesthetically-pleasing space.

The same can apply to our virtual lives. So far, we've focused on simply reducing our time spent scrolling. Today we start to study healthy screen use by "virtual decluttering".

Using tech to manage screen time effectively

We're going to create the digital equivalent of Paolo Coelho's apartment. This way, when you use screens, your environment brings out the best in you.

Scroll hygiene

Starting with some simple scroll hygiene. This is the sort of stuff you already know but may need a reminder of.

- Only have three windows open at once
- Mute your notifications
- In fact, close email when you aren't using it (do you really need to be on it ALL the time?)
- Close tabs. 42 tabs at the top of your screen counts as clutter
- Use folders for a clean and tidy home screen

Then we get into a selection of online services built to help us declutter our devices and the way we use them. They can help us create some of that lovely empty Coelho-like space for focus, attention, downtime, recharging and whatever else.

TIME TO CLEAR UP THAT MESS?

It turns out that clutter has a significant effect on our productivity. Harvard University conducted an experiment on over 100 students and asked them to work in environments with different levels of clutter. The results showed that students who worked in tidy areas worked for more than 50% longer than students working in cluttered areas (1).

Online "scrollutions"

Device Screen Time limits

The native Screen Time controls on the iPhone are unfortunately easily bypassed by a committed scroller like myself. (It simply asks "Ignore Limit?") The Android restrictions can be more effective, but users still report workarounds. I don't recommend either. There are better solutions below.

ScreenZen

This app blocks other apps on your phone that distract and take you away from spending your time productively. *ScreenZen* puts an annoying pause in as you open your most addictive apps. It works well, forcing you to pause and reconsider what you need to do in the moment. I use it on instagram and I curse it every time it delays me from scrolling. I guess that shows it's doing its job.

Limit

Limit is a Google Chrome extension that helps you stay focused on work by restricting the amount of time you can spend on time-wasting scrolling.

Once your allotted time has been used up, the sites you have blocked will be inaccessible for the rest of the day. It shuts down certain websites after a set amount of time. Great for the worst scrolling offenders, plus online activities that masquerade as productive but sap hours from the day (uh, email, we're looking at you).

HeyFocus

Another website blocker for MacBooks. Reclaim your productivity by blocking yourself from scrolling. It also works on games like *Fortnite* (not quite scrolling but highly addictive and a time drain for some). Note: I don't rely on this as, when I'm doing my "best work", I occasionally need the internet for reference, and then I can't access it.

StayFocusd

Yet another browser-based website blocker. This is actually one of my favorites, as it is harder to override. I use this to ban myself from mindlessly scrolling through news sites (doomscrolling is a particular favorite of mine).

Forest

Who doesn't like growing things? *Forest* is an app that helps you stay focused on the important things in life. It is a surprisingly effective app which reframes switching off into something positive. Whenever you want to stay focused, plant a tree. Your tree will grow while you focus on your work. Leaving the app to scroll will cause your tree to wither and die. I like this – when I remember to use it.

Tab Limiter

Tab Limiter (a Google Chrome extension) helps you get scroll control back – by limiting the number of tabs you can open at once. That *Daily Mail* article from three weeks ago that you still had open won't distract you again. You can specify the number of tabs in total and per window. You can also set a customizable message when the tab limit is hit. How about, "my brain has too many tabs open"?

Freedom

Useful for those of us that procrastinate. This is an app and website blocker. You can create a custom blocklist to stop the worst scrolling offenders from taking your attention away from what matters. It enables you to schedule sessions with no distractions. Available on all of your devices.

Here's what I do

I group all my apps into folders on my phone. I obsessively tidy my to-do boards and lists. I use *ScreenZen* every day. I use *Forest* occasionally and always feel good when I've planted a tree. Finally I make generous use of the humble Airplane mode on my phone and, occasionally, laptop too. There is absolutely no way you can be distracted by the internet once they are on.

The final thing that helps me is working on the Underground in London. There's no WiFi there, so I'm forced to concentrate on one thing. Here's a summary of my template for healthy scrolling.

- No more than three tabs open at once.
- Group apps into folders.
- Keep home screens clean, tidy and less scrollable.
- Use other "scrollutions" like *ScreenZen* and *Forest*.

Remember, you want to create the digital equivalent of Paulo Coelho's big, empty apartment with nothing in it.

TO-DO LIST

- ☐ **Switch off for 15 minutes. Recharge.**
- ☐ **Declutter your virtual life. Group apps into folders and close tabs.**
- ☐ **Start using apps like *Forest* or *Freedom* to help you focus.**

DAY 6

Measuring Things

> *"Got my iPhone's weekly Screen Time report and I didn't know I was awake that long."*
>
> – @KyleClark on Twitter

Yeah, you might not be delighted when you look at your Screen Time report. But it is potentially good information that helps us to improve.

In Neuro-Linguistic Programming, we study what works, and then do more of it. And we analyze what's not so good (like a day full of scrolling) and do less of it.

This is why, throughout this program, we measure things.

> *"What's measured improves."*
>
> – Peter Drucker, legendary behavioral change expert

At different points we'll be using screen time reports, accountability buddies, written prompts and the humble to-do list. In this first week, you'll of course have already noticed your daily checklist. This is important, and at the moment, very short (small changes, remember). But it will grow as we advance. As we measure our small daily wins, we hope to start to see correlations between our behavior and how we feel. We also get the satisfaction of putting together a "streak".

You may be feeling ever-so-slightly reluctant to write stuff down. But I emphasize the importance of filling out your to-do list with an actual pen. We are slowly and gently moving small parts of our lives away from screens, and the benefit of using pen and paper (or pen and book) has been well documented by experts such as psychologist James W. Pennebaker. In his work, which has been quoted in multiple studies (1), he observed:

"People who benefit from writing express more optimism, acknowledge negative events, are constructing a meaningful story of their experience, and have the ability to change perspectives as they write."

The kinesthetic sense

In NLP terms, the process of physically picking up a pen and writing something down means we connect to the kinesthetic (touchy-feely) sense that often gets lost when we absorb ourselves in screens. And the benefits can be seen in as small a task as filling out a to-do list.

As you progress through this program and fill out the tick boxes, you'll feel a growing sense of momentum. And look for correlations and ask questions like these:

- On the days when you follow the prompts, do you feel better? Do you have more energy or focus? Are you living your best life?
- On a day when you forget to recharge, is your attention span shorter? Do you feel tired or grumpy?

Some of our measuring methods will change a little as we go, (particularly on Day 15 when we set up accountability buddies), but we'll mostly be using the humble daily checklist.

> If you are reading on a device rather than a paperback, then make sure to note your progress down in an actual notebook, not notes on your phone. This increases the kinesthetic connection.

IS THE PEN MIGHTIER THAN THE SCREEN?

Want to retain information better? Stop scrolling, and start using a pen and paper. A number of studies suggest taking notes on the laptop makes learning harder because it involves shallower information processing.

"The delicate and precisely controlled movements involved in handwriting contribute to the brain's activation patterns related to learning. No evidence of such activation patterns when using a keyboard." (2, 3)

Advanced measuring

A few years ago, being the geek I am, I decided to track what made me feel good each day. I sought out happiness author Gretchen Rubin and spoke to her on my podcast *Zestology*. She believes strongly in measuring things.

> *"Maybe there's something you'd like to change in your life – to get more of something good or less of something bad. Try this: figure out a very concrete way to measure and track it. By counting the things that count – and pushing yourself to find a way to count the things that seem as if they can't be counted – you make sure they're part of your life."*
>
> – Gretchen Rubin, author

So I started a Google spreadsheet. Yes, I'm a spreadsheet guy. I filled it out religiously for the next few months. Then I analyzed the results, and was slightly disappointed. It was actually the obvious stuff – real basics like more sleep – that helped me feel the best.

The information was still useful though. One of the activities that gave me the most energy was exercise. In fact, a workout increased my energy levels by a not inconsiderable 5.4% per day on average.

The more exercise I did, the better I felt. And it didn't have to be strenuous exercise, either. It could be anything from a long walk, to a gym workout or playing tennis with my buddies. All of these different forms of exercise helped me feel good and energized.

It all came about because I started measuring things. I made a simple note of the days when I did exercise. I noticed I felt great on those days. Not a double-blind placebo-controlled study, but good enough for me.

> For advanced metrics, you may want to use spreadsheets like Google Sheets alongside writing stuff down. The results may change your life, even if they aren't scientific.

TO-DO LIST

- ☐ **Switch off for 15 minutes. Recharge.**
- ☐ **Fill out to-do lists and other prompts in this book with a pen to activate optimal neural learning patterns.**

DAY 7

Lock Up Your Cookies

> *"What does it mean that every time I ask my daughter what the best part of her day was, she says 'screen time'?"*
> – Rachel Simmons on Twitter

On my own scrolling journey, I began to wonder about the people around me. How could I gently start a family conversation around screen time limits that wouldn't sound like a dad lecture?

To discuss family boundaries more, I met with *New York Times* bestselling author and productivity consultant, Julie Morgenstern. She wrote the brilliant *Never Check E-mail in the Morning: And Other Unexpected Strategies for Making Your Work Life Work*.

Morgenstern told me that in her 25 years of experience, she's discovered something odd. She found that families who plan to do a particular activity together in the evenings have improved connection, communication and equality within relationships.

And she said it's all about setting firm boundaries around devices. Here are the four areas we explore today.

Screen time boundary suggestions

1. Time boundaries
2. Alternative activities
3. Scroll-free weekends
4. The "If All Else Fails" Option

Time boundaries

When are devices allowed and when are they banned? Does everyone put their devices away in the evening? Are screens allowed until 9pm? Are you a family who take your devices to the bedroom or do you leave them in the kitchen overnight?

I don't like the word "curfew" and so let's not use it. However, defining some boundaries can be very helpful in establishing healthy screen time for everyone.

SMARTPHONE ROLE-MODELING

Good screen habits for kids? Take a look at your own usage first. Research shows children observe and copy what adults do (1). This is known as *overimitation* and the research confirms that overimitation may be a *"universal human trait, unaffected by the age of the child, differences in the testing environment* or *familiarity with the demonstrating adult."*

Translation: how we use our phones is how our kids will use them.

Alternative activities

Julie Morgenstern found that families who do the dishes together get on better. They have improved relationships and communication.

I wondered why doing the dishes – hardly an aspirational or intimate activity – was so key to family relationships? Could this mean that families who do the dishes together stay together? Here's what Morgenstern said.

"Sharing this one simple, daily chore is a gateway to sharing the burden of more complex responsibilities. You'll be spending dedicated time together every day, bonding over a shared meal and shared responsibility to clean up."

Best of all, doing the dishes while scrolling is quite difficult.

Scroll-free weekends

Unfortunately, many people have to be connected throughout the work week, but some still choose a "screen-free" (or as I'm calling it here, "scroll-free") Saturday or Sunday. They often report this as being the best day of their week, and a space for creativity too.

> *"There are times when wisdom cannot be found in the chambers of parliament or the halls of academia but at the unpretentious setting of the kitchen table."*
>
> – E.A. Bucchianeri, author

This – in my experience – only works if you have someone to hold you accountable.

For instance, my family enthusiastically embraced this idea until, one Sunday, we drove to see a friend. Without Waze (a sat-nav app) on my phone, I couldn't get there. And then, of course, the whole thing fell apart once I had switched my phone on. I scrolled through my messages. Then I needed to drive home later in the day. The phone went on again. And the scroll-free day was ruined. Perhaps I should have been more prepared with old-school maps, but I wasn't.

(A final thought on scroll-free weekends. If I had a teenager rather than a toddler they might not be so cool with the idea of switching off all devices until Monday morning.)

> **SCROLL TIPS**
>
> Remember, we are going for tiny changes here to ensure we actually stick to them. Don't get too ambitious with family boundaries. If you turn your house into a no-scroll monastery, it may not stick.
>
> Remember one goal-setting study found 92% of all Americans failed with their resolutions (1). So start small, and turn a goal into a habit.

The "If All Else Fails" option

So you've tried setting boundaries (not curfews) – fail. You've tried doing the dishes together – another fail.

There is another option, but it may not be a popular family boundary.

If you watched the Netflix documentary *The Social Dilemma*, you may have seen a dramatization based on lockable bins. A mom decides the whole family must put their devices in a lockable "kitchen safe." These were originally designed to keep cookies hidden away.

The lockable cookie jar skyrocketed in popularity after that one scene. You can get them from a company called "kSafe." There's no breaking in or cheating with "kSafe." This is the ultimate physical boundary to moderate your scrolling.

So what might be good family boundaries?

To dig into this a bit further I sought out the famous decluttering author Shira Gill. She told me her family switches off their devices at 6:30 p.m. every night. They clear away their dinner, tidy the house and then do something as a family.

Sometimes they go for ice cream, play a game or watch a movie. Yes, a movie does involve a screen. But it doesn't involve multiple screens and it does involve focusing on one thing at a time – clearly a boundary that Shira is willing to accept.

You can listen to more of Shira talking about her family boundaries on *Zestology* episode #334. And, for more inspiration, HealthyChildren.org, from the American Academy of Pediatrics, offers an interactive tool with a family screen time calculator and media plan builder.

TO-DO LIST

- ☐ **Switch off for 15 minutes. Recharge.**
- ☐ **Set family screen time boundaries that work for everyone.**

DAY 8

Alone For The Night

> *"It's almost bedtime, so I'll just check my email, Twitter, Instagram, Facebook, and watch a season of my favorite show on Netflix real quick"*
>
> *— Seen on a T-shirt, London*

Okay, bed-scrollers. Get ready for some science. Studies are finding that people are getting very, very tired from late-night screen use. In just one example, researchers followed 2,000 students based on what they did with their devices at night.

"'Using the mobile for at least 30 minutes... after the lights have been turned off' showed a positive correlation with poor sleep quality, daytime sleepiness, sleep disturbances and increased sleep latency." (1)

I can confess. I'm a bed-scroller by nature. I have to really work at leaving my phone out of my room at night. One of the things that convinced me was that, in this study, students' circadian rhythm (internal body clock) seemed to be affected. That is not good at all. And the researchers had another concern. They were also worried about the electromagnetic field (EMF) implications of sleeping with your phone switched on and near your head.

"'Keeping the mobile near the pillow while sleeping' was also positively correlated with daytime sleepiness, sleep disturbances and increased sleep latency" (2).

Other studies have found the bright light on our devices impacts the depth of our sleep, and our long-term health by suppressing our melatonin levels (3). And another one showed that men who use their phone more in the evenings had a reduced concentration of sperm, as well decreased motility (4).

Studies like this are clearly another reason to quit Netflix/email/Instagram in bed. As we start Week Two, we make a key change to help improve our circadian rhythm.

From tonight: the phone stays out of the bedroom overnight. No more bed-scrolling.

- You now have your alarm clock (with a red filter) that you bought on Day 4
- You have your flashlight (with a red filter) that you bought on Day 4

And that means you are ready. Tonight you'll be going to bed all alone. Well, without your device, anyway.

Did you know that, in China, TikTok is turned off for young users after 10pm? They literally can't access it at bedtime.

So why is this? Technology Ethicist Tristan Harris speculated on his podcast *Your Undivided Attention*. He said, *"TikTok goes dark at 10pm because they realize it might be the opiate for the masses, and they don't want to opiate their kids. Meanwhile they ship the unregulated version of tt to the rest of the world that maximizes influencer culture, narcissism etc. So it's like feeding their own population spinach, while shipping opium to the rest of the world."*

So what's it to be at bedtime? Er, spinach or opium?

Finally, well done on getting to Week Two. We now gently increase the daily amount of time we quit scrolling and recharge instead. You'll notice the checkboxes during the second week reflect this.

TO-DO LIST

- ☐ **Switch off for 30 minutes. Recharge.**
- ☐ **Reclaim your bedtime. All devices stay out of your bedroom.**

DAY 9

Optimal Morning Routine

> *"If you start your day with social media, the news or email, realize that you're starting your day at the mercy of others."*
>
> – Ryan Holiday

Last night, we made a big change to your night-time routine. If you aren't used to sleeping with your phone elsewhere, going cold turkey on bed-scrolling can be tough. I'm speaking from personal experience. But as well as the nighttime benefits, you get a morning boost too.

Let's compare two types of mornings.

1. On the first morning: Scroller Steve wakes up and his phone is next to his bed. He picks it up to check the time, 7:15 a.m. Then he briefly scrolls through his messages (7 messages overnight, 4 already replied to), a news site (some depressing stories), the price of Bitcoin (down!), and Instagram (very amusing post of his friend on vacation, 3 further messages replied to). He puts it down at 7:32 a.m. and gets into the shower.
2. On the second morning: Scroller Steve wakes up and his phone is in a different room. He looks at the alarm clock, 7:15 a.m. He props himself up on the pillows and lies there quietly. He thinks about the day ahead. He has a couple of ideas about what he wants to do at work (and writes something down on the piece of paper next to his bed). He hears some sounds out of the window. He thinks about the

people he loves. He wiggles his toes. He yawns. He takes a deep breath. He opens the curtains at 7:32 a.m. and gets into the shower.

How would you like your mornings to look? When you wake up without a morning screen, here's what tends to happen.

- You wake up naturally.
- The first light you focus on is natural, not artificial.
- You switch your senses on.
- You give your brain sweet space to adjust to the start of the day.

Today, your task is simply to prioritize a natural start to the day. That means

1. **Natural light comes first. The research shows the benefit of morning light to your neural circuits and eyesight.** *"Bright, properly timed light exposures help assure effective circadian photoentrainment and optimal diurnal physiological processes."* **(1)**
2. **If you want to go one better, make sure you go outside in the morning.** *"Artificial lighting is dimmer and less blue-weighted than natural daylight, contributing to age-related losses in unconscious circadian photoreception."* **(2)**

You might feel a little antsy being without your device. I did. You may feel the urge to immediately run to the other room and check your messages when you wake up. Try to allow yourself a few minutes to adjust before you do this – you'll get used to the screen-free mornings soon but it takes a little while. Then you'll reap the benefits: more ideas and thoughts and a clearer-headed start to the day.

Stop Scrolling

TO-DO LIST

- ☐ **Switch off for 30 minutes. Recharge.**
- ☐ **No screens in the bedroom.**
- ☐ **Seek out natural morning light to benefit neural circuits and eyesight.**

DAY 10

Vision Breaks

> "YOUR PHONE IS BLINDING YOU, SCIENTISTS WARN."
>
> – Hyperbolic New York Post headline, August 13th, 2018

I've always prided myself on excellent eyesight. But I have had to concede in recent years that my eyes are simply nowhere near as good as they used to be. I have been trying to convince myself that it's a natural consequence of aging. After all, many people develop presbyopia as they get older (where you gradually lose the ability to focus on close-up objects).

But I've been forced to admit that aging's role is only a small part of the story for me. Because when it comes to the end of a long day in front of my computer, my eyes just don't work as well. Things get a bit blurry. My eyes are tired and overworked.

My eyes are not like this at the start of the day, especially when I spend the whole day chilling, relaxing and away from screens.

I'm not the only one. It seems our eyes are indeed getting worse. And screens are a big part of the problem. A comprehensive review found shocking levels of eyesight issues amongst children because of screens.

> "DES [Digital eye strain] prevalence amongst children alone rose to 50–60% in the COVID-19 era."
>
> – "Digital Eye Strain – A Comprehensive Review", Kirandeep Kaur and others (1)

And eyesight experts have long known that screens are causing issues.

> "You probably notice some uncomfortable effects from staring at your screen too long. Digital-related eye strain affects people of all ages. If you spend hours a day using digital devices, you might notice your vision blurs, and your eyes feel achy and tired. You may also find your eyes become dry, and will tear or sting."
> – American Academy of Ophthalmology" (2)

Most of us are guilty of this, so today, your *Stop Scrolling* task is to use a 20/20 vision break. It combines a simple NLP technique for recalibrating the senses with the American Optometric Association's recommendations for dealing with digital eye strain.

1. Take a very short break every hour to rest your eyes.
2. Look out of the window at something 20 yards away – the optimum distance to give your eyes a rest.
3. Focus for 20 seconds. Notice colors, brightness and movement. Focus solely on this. (No screens).
4. Every time your mind wanders, *start the 20 seconds again*. It may be a surprise how many times you have to start again.

I have found that using 50% blue-light-blocking glasses when using screens means my eyes feel less tired at the end of the day. It is a small but significant improvement. You can buy these from companies like *VivaRays* or *Ocushield*. I tend to use these towards the end of the day.

You can also use eye exercise apps such as *EyeEye* to relieve and recharge your eyes.

By paying attention to your visual field and your attention span, you take a moment to reconnect.

To take this a step further, I sought out the advice of eyesight expert Nathan Oxenfeld from the Integral Eyesight site. We talked on Zoom and he showed me how, every once in a while, he was moving his eyes away from the screen and looking at something further away.

He was switching up the distances at which his eyes were looking to prevent the strain that comes from focusing on one spot very close to you for a long time. Instead he was focusing on a painting on the wall or looking out of the window just past the screen. You can combine this with the NLP technique above.

I am writing this on a plane, and I just shifted my eyes from the screen to the Alps below. Now that's a distance shift of way more than 20 yards! And it felt great to look at the mountains below for a few moments, before shifting my gaze back inside a slightly less lovely airplane cabin.

Let's finish today by returning to the review of children's eyesight and screens. They listed their recommendations out.

"Recommendations to alleviate DES (Digital Eye Strain) include the correct ergonomic use of digital devices, limiting daily screen time to ≤ 4 h, frequent breaks, screen time tracking, blue-light filtering glasses with anti-reflective coating, and an inclination towards outdoor recreational activities" (3)

> ➢ Fewer screens, frequent breaks and more outdoor time. This is good life advice.

Further research: To explore more on eyesight and screens, I have spoken to various top quality natural eyesight experts on my podcast *Zestology*, including; Nathan Oxenfeld (episode #406),

Greg Marsh, (episode #209) Jake Steiner (episode #363), Meir Schneider (episode #368) and Peter Grunwald (episode #347). They all tell some good stories and give excellent examples of how eyesight can be dramatically improved with simple techniques.

TO-DO LIST

- ☐ **Switch off for 30 minutes. Recharge.**
- ☐ **No screens in the bedroom.**
- ☐ **Take regular vision breaks during the day.**

DAY 11

Scroll Apnea

> *"Email apnea – a temporary absence or suspension of breathing, or shallow breathing, while doing email."*
>
> – Linda Stone, February 2008

Linda Stone has impeccable Silicon Valley tech credentials. She was at Apple in the early days. She was a Microsoft vice-president. She was a tech OG. But then she took a left turn. She broke free of that world. Stone became a thinker and writer instead and started to question some of our tech habits. And she began to notice something very strange.

She observed that within the first few minutes of sitting down at her computer, she would start to hold her breath. She would continue to hold it the whole time she was at her screen, even if she did breathing exercises beforehand. She started to wonder, 'Is it just me?'; and the answer was no.

This sparked a six-month investigation of breath-holding and screen time. Stone interviewed over 200 people and was amazed by what she found.

Roughly 80% of this sample appeared to have what she called **email apnea**. Nearly everybody she spoke to held their breath while on their screens.

When I first read this research, I started to tune into my breathing in front of my laptop. Guess what, I too was holding my breath while I was scrolling. You probably do as well. I found this study so compelling, I contacted Stone and set up an interview.

She told me how she had sought out the expertise of a whole variety of healthcare practitioners and researchers on the physiological impacts of breath-holding. It turns out shallow breathing and breath-holding trigger a "fight or flight" response. Basically, bad news.

And we're doing that for hours at a time.

Linda concluded her report by asking these important questions:

"If when we're doing sedentary work, and O2, CO2 and NO are optimally balanced through healthy breathing, will we escape the ravages of an always-on sympathetic nervous system? Can daily breathing exercises contribute to helping reduce asthma, ADD, depression, obesity and a host of other stress-related conditions?"

So do you have, not email apnea but **scroll apnea**?

Today I interrupt your scroll by bringing attention to our breathing.

- Simply being mindful of your breathing is the first step toward countering email apnea. (I just took a deep breath in after writing that.) Set regular reminders. Pause and breathe deeply. Notice how you feel.
- Use breathing apps. (This is making your screen work for you rather than against you). "Othership" is fantastic and has a number of completely free programs.
- One of the things that has helped me in this area is a series of coordinated (or in my case uncoordinated) movements, postures and breath sequences called Qi Gong. It's the breathing element that truly resonates for me; in fact, it makes a significant difference to my day.

Look up *Ha'you Fit* for one of my favorite places to practice these outstanding techniques

---

"Take a deep breath and think of the three things you are grateful for, right in this moment."

– M.J. Ryan, author

To listen to my interview with Linda Stone (she is inspiring and fascinating on many levels), it's on *Zestology* episode #195.

TO-DO LIST

- ☐ **Switch off for 30 minutes. Recharge.**
- ☐ **No screens in the bedroom.**
- ☐ **Get over scroll apnea. Take a moment to breathe.**
- ☐ **Explore breathing apps.**

DAY 12

Taste The Raisin

> "Your screen time has gone up 5995726% since last week. You spent an average of 29 hours a day on your screen. Are you ok?"
>
> – Kristin Noeline, Twitter

During my time with Linda, she explained another concept that she has popularized. The way our minds work is morphing into a state of **continuous partial attention**. Technology is essentially rewiring our brains. She observed that, with continuous partial attention we are now, "always on." And it's not a good thing.

She says, "We're engaged in two activities that both demand cognition. We're talking on the phone and driving. We're writing an email and participating in a conference call. We're carrying on a conversation at dinner and texting under the table on the Blackberry or iPhone."

Living in the moment is hard while scrolling, so today, we are going to work on our attention muscles at a time when we really shouldn't need to scroll anyway – mealtimes.

Stop scroll-munching

There is certainly something counterintuitive in loving food (like I do), planning a meal for hours, and then zombie eating through it while staring at a screen. I confess I sometimes scroll-munch without focusing on the taste, flavors and textures.

Intuitively it feels like a bad habit, but there is now emerging science showing links between screen time and increased body weight, especially in young people (1). In addition, heavy users of screens have been found to have "the least healthful dietary patterns and the poorest health-related characteristics" compared with moderate and light screen users (2). Conversely, mindful eating (i.e., not looking at TikTok while eating), has been shown to combat the tendency to overeat (3), and is highly likely to be associated with weight loss.

Linda Stone found screens at mealtime hinder our parasympathetic nervous system, thus affecting:

"Our sense of hunger and satiety, flow of saliva and digestive enzymes, the relaxation response, and many aspects of healthy organ function."

> Today, no screens when eating. Many of us are guilty of scroll-munching, especially when we are on our own. So put it away. Enjoy your food. Savor the moment.

Joseph B. Nelson provides the brilliant antidote to this to zombie eating by relating Kabat-Zinn's "Raisin Exercise". It's quite long, so here's a small section. This is your task for today, although if you don't have a raisin, feel free to use a blueberry, banana or something else.

1. Look at the raisin and pick it up.
2. Feel its weight.
3. Examine its surface – the various ridges, shiny parts, dull parts; really look for the first time at this strange object.
4. Smell this object and notice how you react.
5. Roll the raisin between your fingers and listen to hear what sound it makes. Notice its stickiness.
6. Notice what you are feeling about this object.

7. Place the raisin between your lips and just hold it there for a few moments. What do you notice happens inside you?
8. Let it roll back into your mouth, but do not chew yet.
9. And so on.

TO-DO LIST

- ☐ **Switch off for 30 minutes. Recharge.**
- ☐ **No screens in the bedroom.**
- ☐ **No scroll-munching or zombie eating. Taste the raisin instead.**

DAY 13

Gray Matter

"Grayscale iPhone ftw"

– @MusAbubaker on Twitter

There is a small but growing movement of people combating screen addiction by turning their phone screens gray. They literally cut all color out of the device screen, and it makes the display boring. That's the idea, anyway, and the science seems to show it actually works by cutting the visual excitement out of your feed.

Grayscale makes scrolling less addictive, reduces anxiety and problematic smartphone use (1).

Let's see if it works for you.

What to do

- Pick up your iPhone and head to Settings (Android has a similar option).
- Then go to Accessibility > Display & Text Size > Color Filters. Switch this on and select Color Tint. Turn the Intensity and Hue dials all the way to gray, then switch off Color Filters again.
- Then go back to Accessibility > Accessibility Shortcut and select Color Filters so there is a tick alongside that option.
- Triple click your home button. Your screen will now be gray. Triple click it again and the gray switches off.

You now have a gray screen to preserve your gray matter. As we've reiterated throughout, there are two aspects to this program. One is reducing our scroll time and the other is managing scrolling and screen time more effectively. Today focuses on the second element.

It's boring but beneficial. Remember, participants in the study above who had their phones in grayscale exhibited a significant decrease in PSU (problematic smartphone use), and anxiety. Importantly, they also reduced their screen time.

I have to talk about my own experience using this. It works well, but I confess, it is something I only use occasionally. It really is almost unbearable looking at a completely gray screen! But grayscale definitely works for me.

Red screen option

Something I do more regularly is turning my phone screen red instead. This cuts nearly all of the blue-light spectrum at night. The purpose is to help my circadian rhythm. If I'm looking at my device in the last couple of hours before bed, I'll simply triple-click three times and reduce my blue-light exposure, plus it makes the device harder to read and to get excited by.

- Go to part 2 of the process above. When you have selected Color Tint, turn the Intensity and Hue dials all the way to red, then follow the rest of the instructions.

Ultimately, both Grayscale and red screen make TikTok, YouTube or Netflix a bit less interesting, especially late at night. And that helps us with scrolling.

TO-DO LIST

- ☐ **Switch off for 30 minutes. Recharge.**
- ☐ **No screens in the bedroom.**
- ☐ **Turn your screen gray to reduce screen time and anxiety.**

DAY 14

The Setback Effect

> *"Being challenged in life is inevitable, being defeated is optional."*
>
> – Roger Crawford

To become a 30 Day Expert, we're making small behavior changes that stick. As we finish our second week, here are two questions:

- Do you have a 100% winning streak on the program so far?
- Have you recharged for 30 minutes every day?

If the answer to either of these questions is *no*, then remember this. Streaks are great, but they don't always happen. Sometimes life gets in the way, or we just have a little lapse. And that's when we need to beware of the "Setback Effect."

Watching out for setbacks

You would think it's unlikely that a single failure would impact your goal. But research shows there's a real danger of missing a day, then getting derailed.

Wenzel et al found that "people are indeed more likely to fail after experiencing an initial instance of failure." This is the "Setback Effect", and their findings note the importance of preparing for setbacks (1). Another source noted a single incident may "affect long-term self-regulation success when people make maladaptive causal attributions to explain their behavior." (2, 3) Unfortunately, we find all sorts of reasons to justify a setback and that means it's more likely we won't reach our goal.

Be resilient. Don't let a setback be the excuse for you to fall back into your old bad habits and deny everything that you've done to make a difference here. 30 days in a row would be epic, but if you don't do it... being resilient is more important.

So as we approach the halfway point of our *30 Day Expert* program, go for that streak, but if you miss a day, be kind to yourself. And get back on it tomorrow.

Dealing with the Setback Effect

1. Go for that streak
2. If you miss a day, be kind to yourself.
3. Cultivate resilience by being mature and realistic.
4. Resolve to renew your commitment tomorrow.
5. Use this as an opportunity to learn and grow.

You may have heard of the *75 Hard* challenge. It is a popular program made up of six "non-negotiable rules" that must be completed for 75 consecutive days. One of the rules is "miss a day, you start again". But what do you think many people do when they hit Day 34 and life gets in the way? Perhaps for some reason they have to miss a day – they get ill, or have 19 meetings back-to-back?

That's right, they won't go back and start again. They'll give up.

➢ Be aware of the Setback Effect and cultivate resilience. You may not need it, but if a day turns up when you have 19 meetings, you'll know it's not the end of the program, and you can rebound tomorrow.

"Life is 10% what happens to you and 90% how you react to it."

– *Charles R. Swindoll*

TO-DO LIST

- ☐ **Switch off for 30 minutes. Recharge.**
- ☐ **No screens in the bedroom.**
- ☐ **Cultivate resilience. Streaks are important. Resilience is more so.**

DAY 15

Slap Screen

> *"This Guy Hired Someone To Slap Him In The Face Every Time He Got On Facebook"*
>
> – Business Insider headline, October 18th, 2012

Over the years I've become friends with productivity expert Maneesh Sethi. Actually, I'm not quite sure the title "productivity expert" does this Stanford graduate justice. He wrote an international bestseller at 14 years old, became a famous DJ in Berlin, founded several companies and is now the CEO of *Pavlok* – a company that produces wearable technology to help you change your habits.

One of the many ways Sethi has grabbed the headlines over the years was when he hired someone to slap him in the face every time he went on Facebook. He had figured out he spent 29 hours a week on Reddit and Facebook, so he posted an ad on Craigslist for someone to be paid $8 an hour to slap him every time he veered off track.

He said it worked. He reported that his productivity instantly increased by 98%. Apparently, it wasn't the fear of the slap that stopped him from checking Facebook; it was the social element of having someone else to help keep him on track.

And so, you will be pleased to hear that we will use the same theory of accountability and support that Maneesh used – minus the slaps. At the start of our third week, we now gently increase our time away from screens to 45 minutes a day. We're also now making use of the latest behavioral science research by making accountability a key part of our *30 Day Expert* program.

Buddy Power

A study on accountability by the Association for Talent Development found the following probabilities of completing a goal at various stages:

- Having an idea or goal: 10% (likely to complete the goal)
- Consciously deciding to do it: 25%
- Deciding when to do it: 40%
- Planning how to do it: 50%
- Committing to someone to do it: 65%
- Having specific appointments with accountability partner: 95%

That's the significance of having an accountability buddy (1).

> Today, I encourage you to set up a messaging group with a friend or ask a buddy to be involved. Yes, I'm aware this involves a screen. As stated from the start, we're both reducing *and* managing our screen time. This includes – at times – using tech to help us, rather than denying its existence.

Now let's set up your scroll time accountability partner (no slaps required).

1. Ask someone to be your accountability buddy (this can be a family member, friend, or anyone).
2. Message them daily with the number of minutes you have switched off your tech and recharged. For instance, June 7th: 30.

That's it. It combines accountability with a more detailed level of tracking. You will end up with extensive data on how long you switch off for, which you can then study by month and even by year. Watch how it makes you more likely to switch off and enjoy recharging.

ABOUT MY ACCOUNTABILITY BUDDY

My accountability buddy is also my wife (awww). A long time ago we set up a group to start measuring how long we meditated for. This works brilliantly and we still use it now. Here's what we do.

- We have a separate WhatsApp group chat and enter the number of minutes we meditate for every day.
- We add up our totals at the end of the month.
- We've "gamified" something we know is good for us. We are competitive, so we want to beat each other.
- Sure, it means we are a bit weird. But we are accountable to each other and it works.

Incidentally, Maneesh's *Pavlok* device is also worth checking out. It's not cheap, but it can help maintain mindfulness, retain focus and practice good habits.

TO-DO LIST

- ☐ **Switch off for 45 minutes. Recharge.**
- ☐ **No screens in the bedroom.**
- ☐ **Get an accountability buddy.**
- ☐ **Message them daily with your total switch off time.**

DAY 16

Sharing Is Caring

> *"What happens on social media stays on social media."*
> – @samueljscott on Twitter

On this 30 Day program, we are interested in lasting behavior change. Today we do something counterintuitive. We harness the power of social media to help us reduce our social media usage. I know it sounds strange, but humans are creatures of habit. We like consistency and we like to be seen as consistent. That means that, when we make a public commitment to something (in person or online), we're more likely to follow through.

FAQ

Q. This sounds a bit weird. You are asking me to go on social media, in a book that is about spending less time on social media.

A. Yes. Think of this as being similar to the famous Tim Ferriss auto-reply he set up in *The 4-Hour Workweek*. People who emailed him received this in reply.

"Due to high workload, I am currently checking and responding to e-mail twice daily at 12: 00 P.M. ET and 4: 00 P.M. ET." (1)

Note - he didn't say he was never going on email again, but he set public boundaries around his usage of it. As the behavioral science below suggests (and I have seen many, many times with clients), making a habit both realistic and public is more likely to make it stick.

- Commitment = Consistency
- The more public the commitment, the more likely we are to see it through.

Ways to make a public commitment

Researchers at Dominican University investigated goal-setting and sharing. They found:

1. Writing your goal down makes it more likely that it will happen.
2. Sharing a goal with a friend makes it even more likely.
3. The best method is to write your goals down, share them, *and* send your friend weekly progress reports (2).

This study shows how the simple pressure to uphold a public commitment can push you to follow through with it. And it is a concept that is easier to unlock than ever, because of social media.

Scroller Steve decides to run a marathon. He enthusiastically tells his friends, who congratulate him and support his decision. Encouraged, he posts on social media and gets lots of hearts and likes. He even collects some early sponsorship.

But two months later, his training hits a brick wall. He's not enjoying long-distance runs. It's cold and boring. It's the middle of winter. He's raised $300 which was less than he had hoped at this stage. And he aches every time he goes out to run in the freezing cold. But how could he possibly give up? He announced he was running the marathon to all his family and friends, and they keep asking how his training is going. It would be embarrassing to give up now.

Scroller Steve was initially driven on because he made a public commitment. Since we know sharing your goals makes them more likely to happen, we are going to go to the place where you can share with a lot of people at once. Social media.

- ➢ Remember, the most powerful way to achieve your goals is to write them down, share them, *and* send weekly progress reports.
- ➢ Now, you can if you like, take this one step further, and notify people on your social accounts about your new online boundaries. *Example: "I'm reducing my scrolling habits and now checking in here once a day. If you see me online at midnight - remind me of this!"*

This plugs in perfectly to the research. And yes, we are now harnessing the power of social media to stop looking at social media. This is where things get a bit meta. But the Law of Commitment will click into action as you announce to the world that you are developing healthy screen time habits. You will be plugging into powerful, research-proven behavioral science.

Of course this sounds counterintuitive. But we've already said we don't want to deny the existence of social media. We want to use it mindfully to help enhance our lives, not deplete them.

Back to Scroller Steve. Four months later, he crossed the finish line of the London Marathon, his arms aloft and his face etched with triumph and pain. He had endured the desperate depths of winter. But he didn't want to let his friends down. Once he posted on social media, it made him more likely to follow through on his goal. That's how he completed the marathon, and that's the power of commitment and consistency for you.

TO-DO LIST

- ☐ Switch off for 45 minutes. Recharge.
- ☐ No screens in the bedroom.
- ☐ Use social media to help you quit social media with The Law Of Commitment.

DAY 17

Movement Snacks

> *"When people run around – or engage in any form of exercise – their ability to pay attention improves."*
>
> – Johann Hari, Stolen Focus

The likelihood is that you spend too much time on your bum. You are reading this book about screens, after all. The antidote is movement. Not only is there a clear mood and health uplift from getting away from your screens, but it also helps with attention span and longevity.

I have extensively studied supercentenarians who lead healthy, active lives. I've found that constant low-level exercise was one of the secrets of their old age. I then compared their lifestyle to people who work on computers, especially at home (WFHers). I didn't need to be Sherlock Holmes to discover two things.

- Supercentenarians walk all day and hardly ever look at screens.
- We look at screens all day and hardly ever walk.

This is the great Working From Home (WFH) Problem. We sit at home and are trapped at our desks. We scroll through endless emails. We stare into a screen all day. I'm sitting at home right now writing this. I know it is not good for me. Studies find that working from home is associated with more time sitting down, which is negatively associated with health and well-being (1). It is also proven that physically active individuals are less likely to suffer from depressive symptoms. Conversely, those who spend more time on screens have a worse mental health status (2).

Today, your task is to take "movement snacks" throughout the day. Remember, the more you exercise, the better your attention will be. The better your attention is, the less likely you will be to aimlessly scroll. It'll be a virtuous circle.

So how can you design your work around fewer screens and more movement? Here is some inspiration that may help, though you may just sometimes have to put the laptop away and get outside.

- **Move chairs away from your desk.** This means you have to stand up more.
- **Leave your trainers by the door.** This encourages you to exercise. (In my experience this is brilliant for a few days, and then stops working, but it might work better for you!)
- **Have walking meetings.**
- **Do any work you can while moving.** I've experimented with replying to emails on the treadmill in the gym. It's not the deepest work ever but I'm on the move and it feels good.
- **Buy a good umbrella.** This may not seem to qualify as a top tip, but I bought a good umbrella so I can walk in the London rain. It gets used often. I'll come back from a walk on a damp day with a boosted mood. I walk obsessively now, come rain or shine.

Here's how I do it. My company instigated a rule in week one: All meetings were to be walking meetings. We now genuinely look forward to meetings. We do them either in person strolling around the office or, if we are working from home we'll put headphones on and just start walking around as we talk. A nice by-product is that we also tend to solve problems in these meetings better.

We did come upon a problem. Sometimes, people don't want to do walking meetings. They want to show you something, or present something, or they need to consult notes or a computer or any number of things.

That's fine. We adapted our rule so that we just do walking meetings when we can.

I know movement snacks may be a challenge for you. I know you may have a boss who thinks this is crazy. I get it. We are going for small changes. A life with fewer screens is a simpler one, and research shows it's better for you.

One more point on scrolling and posture. Guess what – it turns out that the ever-increasing army of devices we own is causing increasing numbers of neck problems. The term "Text Neck" refers to frequent forward neck flexion when looking at mobiles.

And according to the doctor who invented the phrase, we need to watch out for this problem with all our devices, not just with hand-held scrolling.

"Text Neck is not just a texting problem," says Dr. Dean Fishman. *"Text Neck is a gaming problem. Text Neck is an e-mailing problem."* (2)

We slump in our chairs or we lean over the kitchen table, shoulders hunched over our computer, and our bodies become inflamed as a result.

Netflix Neck

During the first Covid lockdown, I spent all day working on my laptop on the sofa in a terrible position. Then my wife and I indulged in some epic Netflix binges. (I confess, I did not follow the "no screens in the bedroom rule" in this period. Because of the exceptional circumstances, we decided it would be cozy to do this in bed, so we watched hours at a time on a laptop in the bedroom.)

My neck was getting increasingly sore during the day and I couldn't figure out why. It turned out that lying like this with my head jammed slightly forward was putting a huge amount of extra pressure on my neck. Was this the first ever case of Netflix Neck? Probably not.

WATCH OUT FOR THE CLAW

Other scroll-related injuries and issues include:

- Text Claw: soreness and cramping in the fingers from, er, too much texting
- Cyber Sickness: motion sickness from looking at screens too much
- Computer Eye: digital eye strain (see Day 10)
- Phantom Vibe: imagining your phone is vibrating in your pocket when it's not

---

Just reading this has probably made you sit up straighter. Other potential solutions to Text Neck are a good ergonomic office chair, a cheap stand for your laptop which elevates the height of the screen and therefore raises your neck (mine cost less than $15 and I'm writing on it now), and of course, all the above about putting the screens down and getting moving.

Movement is primitive. We need it and we don't get enough of it when we WFH.

TO-DO LIST

- ☐ **Switch off for 45 minutes. Recharge.**
- ☐ **No screens in the bedroom.**
- ☐ **Take regular movement snacks, buy an umbrella, and beware of Text Neck.**

DAY 18

Creative Quietude

> "My best ideas come in the shower, where I'm showered with water, but also ideas."
> – Ryan Lilly

How often do you get good ideas while taking a shower? For many people, good ideas seem to happen there – where there are no distractions.

There are even scientific theories on Shower Thoughts (1). Harvard researcher Shelley H. Carson recognized the way an "incubation period" plays a part in our creativity. Jumping into the shower is thought to be an incubation period, "in other words, a distraction may provide the break you need to disengage from a fixation on the ineffective solution."

Mark Fenske, co-author of *The Winner's Brain* and an associate professor of neuroscience at the University of Guelph in Canada notes that, because "shampooing hair and lathering up doesn't take a lot of cognitive focus, other parts of the brain can start to contribute." (2)

We now embark on two days of slowing down, and escaping the scroll, to encourage, if not quite Shower Thoughts, at least Slower Thoughts.

Lao-Tzu, the Chinese Taoist philosopher, taught a principle known as "Creative Quietude" through which one could accomplish great things without appearing to work hard for them. To me, this is a valuable lesson worth pursuing. Because our deepest moments of inspiration don't come when we are rushing around, checking the iPhone, occupying our mind with TV, video, phone, email, Facebook, or anything else. Our moments of inspiration come in quiet moments of deep thought. Like, er, in the shower

So in this busy day and age, I would like you to borrow from Lao Tzu whenever you want a jolt of inspiration. He said:

"We can clarify troubled waters by slowly quieting them."

He also said,

"Silence is a source of great strength."

But how do you find that rare moment of quietude, from which inspiration and creativity may come?

It has to come during those idler moments. It may be through sitting quietly, reading, yoga, walking, or massage. Or perhaps it will be in the shower. Somewhere without distraction.

> Today's task is to indulge in a few moments of creative quietude/mind wandering. This gives you an excellent excuse to sit on the sofa doing not very much. Our minds need a little downtime to cope with all the uptime.

Lao Tzu taught that all straining and striving is not only vain, but also counterproductive. One should aim for inner tranquility. From there comes spontaneity and creativity. Easier said than done for a Type A personality like me, but we will give it a go!

> **QUIZ TIME**
>
> Here's a little quiz. How busy a person are you?
>
> A. You'll normally find me with my feet up, without a care in the world, reading my book and looking forward to a chilled glass of something nice later on.
> B. I love to relax, but often I simply schedule too much into my day. I wish I had more time, but that's the same as everyone, right?
> C. I'm a worker. When I'm not working hard, I feel anxious. Finding the time to read this book is a struggle and makes me guilty, as I should be doing something more productive.

If you answered A, then lucky you. Enjoy your chilled glass of something nice. If you answered B or C, then you're like the vast majority of people I speak to (and me). The truth is, our minds need a little downtime to cope with all the uptime.

Here's one more modern take on downtime, from Tim Kreider in the *New York Times*.

"Idleness is not just a vacation, an indulgence or a vice; it is as indispensable to the brain as vitamin D is to the body."

TO-DO LIST

- ☐ **Switch off for 45 minutes. Recharge.**
- ☐ **No screens in the bedroom.**
- ☐ **Cultivate inspiration and "quietude". Maybe in the shower.**

DAY 19

Be More Jobs

> *"My favorite things in life don't cost any money. It's really clear that the most precious resource we all have is time."*
> – Steve Jobs

"Modeling" means studying ourselves as well as other people and applying what works to our own lives. By observing, and sometimes copying the ways others achieve results, we can start to learn from them and improve ourselves.

This might be the most important Neuro-Linguistic Programming skill. Sometimes, I like to think of NLP as an umbrella term for all sorts of helpful tools whose effectiveness has been proven by science, and that can really help us with behavior change. Modeling is one such tool. Social cognitive psychologist Albert Bandura greatly influenced NLP; in 1977 he explained,

> *"Most human behavior is learned observationally through modeling: from observing others one forms an idea of how new behaviors are performed, and on later occasions, this coded information serves as a guide for action."*
> – Albert Bandura, Social Learning Theory

In NLP, Bandler et al expanded on this theory and created their modeling technique. Here's how you can model healthy tech usage.

NLP Modeling

- Identify someone who has skills, achievements or successes that you would like to replicate. (For example, somebody who is great at switching off, or seems very present around their phone, or is super creative.)
- It can be somebody famous, or somebody well known in their field, or someone you know personally.
- Approach them if you can, and ask questions. Otherwise, read about them and study them.
- Don't copy them. Instead take an aspect of their environment, behavior, capabilities, values, beliefs or identity and apply the relevant points to your life.

I use this in every area of my life. When I want to learn something new, I find someone who is good at it, and learn from them. For example, I'm learning Padel Tennis. It's the fastest-growing sport in the world and a fun form of small court tennis. I'm gradually trying to acquire the skills of the top Padel players by reading about them and watching them. It's a very slow process – despite having been a sports TV presenter for many years I am not a natural sportsman – but it is satisfying to learn from outstanding players and improve in this way.

When it comes to screens, one of the people I've enjoyed modeling is, ironically, someone who was probably more responsible for scroll addiction than most of us. Steve Jobs invented the iPhone, but was pretty good at switching off and recharging himself.

"If you just sit and observe, you will see how restless your mind is. If you try to calm it, it only makes it worse, but over time it does calm, and when it does, there's room to hear more subtle things – that's when your intuition starts to blossom and you start to see things more clearly and be in the present more. Your mind just slows down, and you see

a tremendous expanse at the moment. You see so much more than you could see before."

— *Steve Jobs*

I have found it useful to learn from this, and sit and observe, Steve-Jobs-like, for at least a few minutes a day. Does my intuition blossom? Can I hear subtle things? What comes into my consciousness that I wasn't aware of before? Does inspiration spring from an unexpected place?

So that's how I use modeling. Remember, it is not about trying to copy someone else, or saying that one individual had all the answers. It is about acknowledging that we can learn from certain aspects of other people and their approach to life. And we can see if we can apply some of their wisdom to our own lives. Like Jobs' thoughts on slowing the mind.

> ➤ Your task today is to replicate Jobs' approach to "see so much more than you could see before."

TO-DO LIST

- ☐ **Switch off for 45 minutes. Recharge.**
- ☐ **No screens in the bedroom.**
- ☐ **Learn from others using the NLP modeling technique.**

DAY 20

Micro Reminders

> *I love technology but we've got generations that have started living virtually. They're watching people live their lives instead of living their own lives, and that's changed everything.*
>
> *– Dr. Phil*

Scroller Steve thought this program was a great idea. But here we are on Day 20, and the bad habits are creeping back in. In fact, right now he's sitting on the toilet and living up to his name, scrolling through his feed while simultaneously cleaning his teeth, cutting his nails and listening to a podcast.

We are learning to live with tech in a healthy way. We don't want to deny its existence. So for the next two days, let's get playful with our devices to provide little micro-reminders of when we are trying to do six things at once.

Today we will set up a little screen reminder, or, in NLP terminology, a "Pattern Interrupt." It works by interrupting a pattern of behavior or thoughts, and it is an effective measure for behavior change.

First, write down your program goal on this page. As we've already explored, science shows we're more likely to do something when it is written down by hand (1). Write it in 10 words or less. Focus on what habits you will have established when you've become a 30 Day Expert. Write it in the present, as if it's already happened and give it the date of whenever you'll reach Day 30.

Stop Scrolling

My goal:

_____

_____

Date:

_____

Example:

My goal:

More recharging. More nature. I feel more relaxed and calm.

Date

June 1st

This is a powerful way of manifesting. Rather than just talking about it, you articulate your new habit, and focus on how you will feel and the emotion behind it.

Screensavers = Micro reminders

Now we set up a little micro-reminder of your goal to display every time you tap your phone.

- Take a photo of the page.
- Set it as your lock screen and home screen.

You can change your screensaver regularly to represent your goal, and it doesn't have to be words.

For instance, today I opened up my phone and saw a picture of a Scottish glen. In front of the glen, someone is holding a camera lens, through which I can see a very focused part of the glen. This picture represents my goal for this 30 Day program. It represents the expertise that I want to achieve, and it embodies the idea that I want more focus.

I regularly change these pictures and backgrounds, and not just on my mobile phone. In fact, on Trello (a useful online system of boards, lists and cards), I change my background almost every day to represent different goals. I put up all kinds of colors, quotes and inspiring images. That way my brain doesn't acclimatize to the same picture and then ignore it. Here's how my Daily Planner looks today.

I want to emphasize the idea that, while this may seem an almost trite way to help with goal-setting, pattern interrupts really work.

These micro-reminders provide an interruption to remind us of our destination.

> **QUIT DOOMSCROLLING WITH PATTERN INTERRUPTS**
>
> "My life has been so much better since I quit doomscrolling all the time."
>
> – Real_NoobToob on Urban Dictionary
>
> Doomscrolling is a term that describes the obsessive urge to scroll through negative news. It's hard to stop, especially when the news is depressing. We all did so much doomscrolling when the Covid pandemic first struck that the word entered the Oxford English Dictionary and was named a word of the year.
>
> Pattern interrupts are particularly helpful if you are addicted to reading endless bad news. I prefer an unsubtle approach.

> ➤ **Write STOP DOOMSCROLLING on a post-it note. Then take a picture of it and set it as your screensaver. That is the unsubtle (but effective) pattern interrupt that helps me quit reading bad news.**

Remember, a pattern interrupt is anything that *interrupts your pattern*; they can be found or created everywhere. Actually, we've explored these already. Remember, for example, the browser-based website blockers we used on Day 3? The ones that stop you mindlessly scrolling are using a classic pattern interrupt.

- Your pattern is to mindlessly go to your favorite website and scroll.
- Your pattern is interrupted when you are blocked from visiting it.

I use pattern interrupts all the time, from my passwords to my screensavers.

TO-DO LIST

- ☐ **Switch off for 45 minutes. Recharge.**
- ☐ **No screens in the bedroom.**
- ☐ **Use a "pattern interrupt" on your lock screen for healthier screen habits.**

DAY 21

Screen Time to Green Time

> *"There is no WiFi in the forest but I promise you will have a better connection."*
>
> – Sharon Bannister

Our brains link visual stimuli to thoughts and emotions, particularly when it comes to different colors (1). From a behavioral science perspective, we can use this knowledge to help reduce our dependence on screens and scrolling.

For instance:

- Blue: The color of the ocean and the sky. It is associated with calm, peacefulness and happiness.
- Green: The color of nature. The science shows it is relaxing and soothing. Hospitals often paint walls light green because it is comforting for patients.
- Yellow: Studies have associated this color with flowers, happiness and rainbows (but also vomit and sickness!)
- Red: The most emotionally intense color. It can be associated with excitement, confidence, power and also fear.

Today we focus on green, as there is some particularly compelling science around this color. Research suggests when you go outside and surround yourself with greenery, you'll be happier and healthier. So far, so obvious. But it turns out you don't necessarily need to go outside to achieve this.

Author Oliver Burkeman has observed that:

1. In a university building, workers on the greenery side took 19% fewer sick days.
2. Pupils do worse in tests in windowless classrooms.
3. Hospital patients are discharged more quickly when they're in a room with a view.

And the research takes an unexpected turn.

Simply looking at a picture of greenery for a couple of seconds leads to improvements in relaxation and a reduction in stress.

Researchers in the Netherlands showed participants a series of pictures, some of which had greenery in them. When they looked at the nature images, their stress levels reduced thanks to the activation of their parasympathetic nervous system (which relaxed their bodies) (2).

Let's try a similar experiment now. Look at these pictures for yourself and see if you feel differently when you look at;

- Picture 1 (the view from my room on holiday)
- Picture 2 (the view from a London street near me) tk

Stop Scrolling

NLP teaches us that the brain struggles to perceive the difference between real and imagined experience, which is perhaps why the science works this way.

We have already acknowledged that we are not going to live in a scroll-free world. We will still be picking up our devices and scrolling in future; we will just be doing it more mindfully.

Today's task helps us to use behavioral science to feel better while we pick up or switch on our devices.

> ➤ You last changed your screensaver on Day 3. Now it's time to change it again. Switch your screensaver to a natural, green view. Pick a picture that you took yourself, or choose

a nice relaxing green view you can find online. Remember, our brains link thoughts and emotions to colors, so we use this to provide a healthier screen environment.

TO-DO LIST

- ☐ **Switch off for 45 minutes. Recharge.**
- ☐ **No screens in the bedroom.**
- ☐ **Change your screensaver and feel better when you scroll.**

DAY 22

Blocking Sites

> *"Are you OK? I haven't seen you post a selfie in the last five minutes?"*
>
> *– Unknown*

We've already looked at some of the screen time tools that exist to help us limit certain apps and sites. But these scroll-limiters, to be blunt, don't always work that well.

The problem is this. There is no major incentive for device manufacturers to actually be strict and allow us to switch off. It goes against the business model for us to be able to put down our phone, go out and, ya know, actually interact with others in person.

Let me demonstrate with the iPhone. Now, I'm an iPhone fanboy. But its Screen Time feature sucks.

1. **In theory:** Screen Time allows us to control excessive screen usage. We can view our weekly stats, identify problem areas, and then limit our usage of those sites, apps and areas. It encourages us to spend less time on digital devices.
2. **In practice:** I check my last week of Screen Time stats. My iPhone tells me I spent a lot of time on Instagram. I decide to set a 20 minute Insta limit. After 20 minutes of use a notification pops up saying "You've reached your limit on Instagram". At the bottom of the screen, a blue button says "Ignore Limit". I click on it, and go back to using Instagram. With the tap of a button, I am able to override the feature designed to moderate my screen time. *And I always do.*

So, I can confirm from personal experience that the Screen Time controls on the iPhone are not effective. Some devices do have more powerful screen time options, like *Gabb* and *The Light Phone* (see Day 28 for details).

If your device makes it easy to set limits with no override, fantastic – set them.
If your device makes it difficult to set scroll limits that stick, read on.

This is a fantastic workaround for the iPhone, and other devices have similar features.

- Go to Screen Time > Content & Privacy Restrictions > Content Restrictions > Web Content
- Click on Limit Adult Websites
- Add websites you want to limit.
- Delete related apps.

Now my phone won't let me scroll through Twitter because it thinks that it is "adult content". I can't open it at all.

In fact, you still can override these content restrictions, but it involves a lot of clicks and completely changing your parental controls. You're less likely to go through the whole process than click a simple button that says "ignore limit". It is admittedly ridiculous to have to go to these lengths to limit certain kryptonite sites but that is the world of screens we live in.

TO-DO LIST

- ☐ **Switch off for one hour. Recharge.**
- ☐ **No screens in the bedroom.**
- ☐ **Use content restrictions to permanently block addictive sites and apps.**

DAY 23

Are You An E-voider?

> *"You Now Have a Shorter Attention Span Than a Goldfish."*
> – Kevin McSpadden

We spoke previously about the tool known as the "pattern interrupt". It works by interrupting a pattern of behavior or thoughts, and in NLP, it is often used as a positive agent for behavior change. But unfortunately, it's not always a good thing. In fact, the pattern interrupt is being used against us all day every day on our screens. The *New York Times* reported that the average human attention span is now 8.25 seconds, and the average goldfish attention span is 9 seconds (1). So do we really have a shorter attention span than a goldfish?

On average, we pick up our phone 1,500 times a week, and much of it is because our attention is being interrupted (2).

When you receive a notification, you are receiving one of these pattern interrupts.

This may seem simple and obvious – and it is. But the ways in which notifications cause pattern interrupts are becoming ever more sophisticated. And that's why action is needed. Clearly, there are some things we can't change about the addictiveness of our devices. But notifications make it easier to return to the scroll, and we have the power to switch them off.

- Ping! They draw you back to your screen.

- Ping! They shorten your attention span.
- Ping! They make it harder to recharge.
- Ping! They interrupt your behavior, and ask you to context-switch (which is mentally tiring).
- Ping! They load you with extra information (which is also tiring).
- Ping! They encourage an addiction to instant gratification (which is not helpful).
- Ping! The average attention span is now 8.25 seconds.

How could I write this book if I had all my notifications on and continued to receive messages about large animals on public transport? I probably could write it, but it would take a very long time.

Here's how we fight the pattern interrupts and focus for longer than 8.25 seconds. We simply control what we can on our devices.

E-void everything non-essential by switching off all notifications on all devices.

> *"You can try having self-control, but there are a thousand engineers on the other side of the screen working against you."*
>
> *– Tristan Harris, former Google engineer and technology ethicist, testifying before the US Senate.*

Self-control is easier when notifications are switched off.

E-voiding can include:

- Lock screen notifications
- Banners
- Sounds
- Vibrations
- Alerts

- Badges, and of course…
- Pings

> **IT'S NOT RUDE TO E-VOID**
>
> E-voiding is the Urban Dictionary definition for avoiding someone electronically.
>
> It's simple. E-void them now, reply later. Otherwise you're suffering from continuous partial attention, and you'll never get anything done.*
>
> E-voiding is not rude; in fact, it is an essential tool if you're trying to work, be creative, think or get things done.
>
> So get involved in guilt-free e-voiding today.

Notifications dilute our attention. They make it weaker. In a brilliant study called, *The attentional cost of receiving a cell phone notification,* it was shown notifications "can prompt task-irrelevant thoughts, or mind wandering, which has been shown to damage task performance". Even when participants did not use their phones during the task, the negative impact of notifications is comparable with users actively using their phone (1).

In addition, notifications have a strange effect on our brains. In another study, 89% of undergraduates experienced 'Phantom vibration syndrome' (2). This means thinking your pocket is vibrating when it's not. So it's really worth getting your notification game right. Even if you think your notification settings are on point, they may not be.

I have just checked mine again after writing this. Quite a few of the recent apps I've downloaded seem to have automatically enabled notifications. So I unchecked all the boxes again. Is it time for you to do another stocktake on all devices too?

> *"Turn off all notifications on your phone, except the most important ones. And check your social media only once or twice a day, not every minute. If you can do this, then perhaps there is a possibility, that society will not completely lose its sanity and health after all."*
>
> – Abhijit Naskar, Neuroscientist

TO-DO LIST

- ☐ **Switch off for one hour. Recharge.**
- ☐ **No screens in the bedroom.**
- ☐ **E-void all notifications by changing your settings (screen and sound).**

DAY 24

Supplements

> *"...a lot of people don't know that one of the major side effects of CBD oil is having to constantly remind people that you use CBD oil."*
>
> – @Dxxnya on Twitter

My *30 Day Expert* programs make use of behavioral science, NLP and also cutting-edge biohacking tools. Biohacking is getting the best out of your body and life by adapting your environment, lifestyle and diet, so it fits in great with the theme of scrolling. Sometimes it involves gadgets, tech and supplements to help you get back to or to mimic a more primal natural state, which can be hard otherwise. For instance, it's very natural to sunbathe, but when you're sitting at a desk all day you might not be getting much good quality light, therefore some time in front of an infrared light can help.

Biohacking can be particularly helpful when it comes to diet– and natural supplements, when diet isn't enough. Using natural supplements (not pharmaceuticals) has become a common theme that has emerged from my years of looking into nutrition and energy. With these supplements, we can fill in the gaps.

Since you are approaching expert level in this 30 day program, today we look at how a protocol that includes highly targeted natural supplements could help you be less distracted. But what makes this relevant to our scrolling habits? We are trying to boost our focus, attention span, energy and resilience with healthy screen use, and good nutrition can significantly help with that.

DISCLAIMER

I'm a journalist and author, not a doctor (and I don't want to be one). The following is for informational purposes only, and you should run any new health regime past your doctor or health practitioner.

CBD

Are you just a bit too jacked up, even when you step away from the screen?

CBD is Cannabidiol, one of the most naturally abundant compounds found in the hemp plant. It is not psychoactive (unlike THC). I find CBD chills me out and provides a nice antidote to that "always-on" feeling that comes from spending way too long in front of my laptop. It also helps with sleep and relaxation.

Only use very pure, organic brands, derived from a specific strain of the hemp plant. It is one of many cannabinoids in hemp that have a variety of effects on our body.

I now use CBD on some evenings (around an hour before bed) to unwind after a long day of screen use. I occasionally use it during the day too, for relaxation or to "get into the zone".

Start with low doses and gently increase until you find your own tolerance level. These vary wildly from person to person. (My tolerance level is very high, but some people would zonk out if they had as much as I do. If yours is much lower, that's great as it works out a lot cheaper that way.)

Try taking it: in the evening to unwind; half an hour prior to recharging; or to "take the edge off" when doing something very mentally stimulating.

Blue Cannatine

There is a powerful blue pill that instantly changes the way you feel (no, not Viagra). It helps with focus and energy, and... turns your tongue blue. In fact, it turns your mouth so blue they call it the "smurf pill".

Blue Cannatine users have reported an increase in mental performance, focus, clarity, energy, and effective workouts – and no jitters.

It really does work and I use it on an occasional basis – although it is quite expensive. This supplement is powerful, and contains a number of strong performance enhancers including

- Nicotine
- Caffeine
- Methylene blue

It can help with better memory, focus and mood and is proven to be safe at the dosage level present in Blue Cannatine. And it turns out nicotine isn't as bad for you as you thought (although smoking definitely is.)

You can also look for nicotine gums or sprays to help with coordination, vigilance, memory and reaction speed. I personally find these too high-dose. In Blue Cannatine, the nicotine is at a lower dose than most other supplements.

Try taking it immediately before focused screen time.

Adrenal support

In my old job as a TV journalist, I'd often finish on air at midnight. Then I'd drive home, and then... I'd look at screens again, often until 4am or 5am. Then I'd go to bed and wake up bleary-eyed about 11am. What was I thinking? Crazy, I know. I'm a reformed screen addict for sure.

> If you too have spent years looking at screens until late at night, you may have neglected your health, focus and adrenal system. You may need more specialized help from an experienced functional practitioner. They may recommend supplements to help.

I have found targeted adrenal supplements helpful. I really like Dr. Ben Lynch's *Seeking Health* supplements for adrenal support. If you think your adrenals might be being taxed by all the stimulation and stress from screens, then check out his products, in particular *Optimal Adrenal* and *Adrenal Cortex* (which is especially powerful).

Again, this is my experience only. Consult with your doc or practitioner before embarking on supplementation to check it's right for you.

TO-DO LIST

- ☐ **Switch off for one hour. Recharge.**
- ☐ **No screens in the bedroom.**
- ☐ **Explore supplements to increase focus or unwind after a long online session.**

DAY 25

Logical Levels

> "No iPad. You guys have had plenty of screen time today!' she shouts, without looking up from her phone."
>
> – @MyMomologue on Twitter

I was with my friend Anna yesterday. She has an 18-month-old toddler. She told me that she's caught herself a few times doing something she really doesn't want to do while looking after her little one.

Yep. Scrolling.

Her toddler will be engaged in a game or wanting her attention and Anna will find herself on her phone, checking a message or idly scrolling. (As the parent of a young, boisterous boy, I empathize with Anna. Sometimes it's hard to muster the enthusiasm to play "cars" for the hundredth time, however sweet the game is.)

So Anna thought about it. And used these words:

"That's not my values. That's not who I am. I've got to change that. I've got to put the phone down and put the phone away when I'm with my 18-month-old son."

What are your values?

Logical Levels was invented by a brilliant NLP Trainer called Robert Dilts. Using it, we can assess what's going on at every level of our life, including our habits around screens. I've adapted it to look like this.

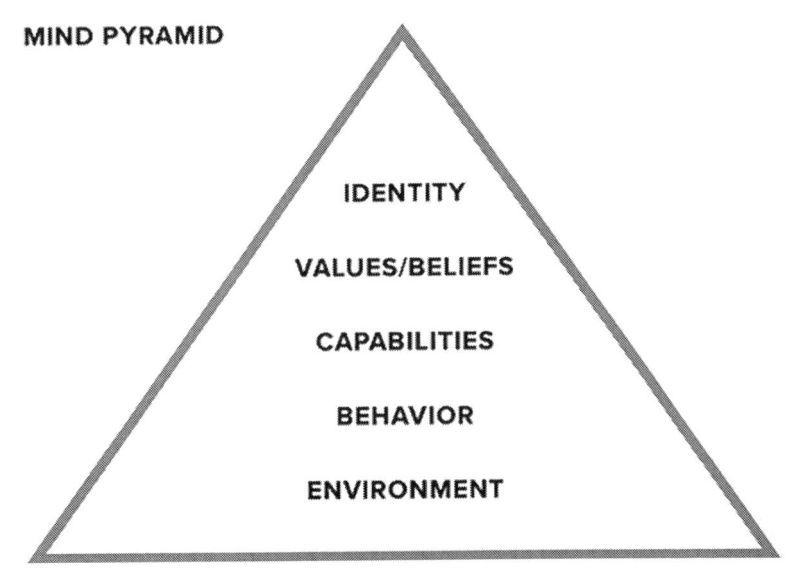

MIND PYRAMID

- IDENTITY
- VALUES/BELIEFS
- CAPABILITIES
- BEHAVIOR
- ENVIRONMENT

Throughout this program, we have mostly been at the bottom of the pyramid. We have mainly changed our *environment*, and *behavior* around screens and scrolling.

But it's often useful to travel up to the complex levels at the top of the pyramid.

Your task today is to mull over these questions and consider your answers. It may take a while. This is definitely an exercise to do during recharging.

- Who am I as a person?
- What do I believe is important about how I live my life?
- What are my values?
- What do I believe is important about my identity?

(Note: The questions may not seem related to screen use, but they most certainly are.)

> When you start to think about those questions, and maybe even write something down, it gives you interesting insights. A strong awareness of your values and beliefs leads to positive changes in behavior and environment.

For example, Anna is reminded of her strong value that she wants to be present with her young son, it means she will alter her behavior to scroll less, and she might change up her environment by putting her phone in the other room while playing with him.

TO-DO LIST

- ☐ **Switch off for one hour. Recharge.**
- ☐ **No screens in the bedroom.**
- ☐ **Consider your values/beliefs around screen use. This can help with behavior change.**

DAY 26

Task Batching

> *"The more you multitask, the less deliberative you become; the less able to think and reason out a problem."*
>
> – Nicholas Carr

We already know that we find "distractions more distracting" when our brains are overtaxed. Multitasking makes this worse, and most of us are now world-class multi-taskers on our devices. We scroll while we wait for the lift. We walk down the street while sending messages. We read our emails sitting on the toilet. One in 10 people even admit to checking their phones during sex (1).

We clearly need help.

Task batching

Task-batching is grouping similar tasks together, then doing them all together in one go, rather than bit-by-bit over the course of the day.

For instance, you might batch all your emails together at 9am, 1pm and 5pm.

Why does this work? Our brains aren't meant to multi-task. In fact we're not very good at it. So task-batching takes advantage of flow state. Your brain is taxed less, as it isn't context-switching all day. There's a place in the day for deep work (nope, Instagram not allowed), then a place in the day for emails, for messaging, checking the football scores and, yes, maybe some Insta time too.

> **LOSING TIME**
>
> In 2001, researchers carried out a fascinating series of experiments around multitasking. Participants were asked to switch between tasks such as solving math problems or classifying geometric objects. The researchers found:
>
> - Switching between different tasks slows people down and creates "mental blocks".
> - More time was lost as the tasks got more complex.
> - Time costs were greater when switching to unfamiliar tasks.
>
> The more you switch between different, complex tasks, the slower you will be. The study noted that "even brief mental blocks created by shifting between tasks can cost as much as 40 per cent of someone's productive time." (1)

Here's how task-batching works for me. Firstly, when writing, I do nothing else. No other tasks are allowed. It's the only way I can focus properly.

Then I manage my daily to-do list with task-batching. I use Trello (an online system of boards, lists and cards) to batch things together as efficiently as possible. I have a "work to-do" list, a "work watching" list, and a "personal to-do" list.

I'll group similar tasks together, then do them all at once. For instance, on Tuesdays I record podcasts. On Mondays I spend a certain amount of time writing. And I batch non-urgent tasks too. On my personal to-do list today, I've got some potentially distracting tasks that I need to get done...

- Pay a parking ticket

- Book a Padel Tennis court for Friday
- Order a new toilet plunger on Amazon (exciting!)

I will batch these non-urgent tasks into one area of my to-do list, for one portion of the day. Then I'll return to a more disciplined deep-work headspace to continue writing this book until it's time to switch tasks.

Now it's your turn.

Help with Task Batching

1. Pick a to-do list program/app like todoist (no-frills, very effective) or Trello (more advanced, my personal favorite)
2. Put all your tasks and to-dos in there.
3. Batch them up. Make use of tags, categories and lists to batch tasks together

➤ Task-batching can: make your screen time more focused; improve productivity; help you stay on top of your to-do list; and (most importantly) help you kick your mindless scrolling habit.

TO-DO LIST

- ☐ **Switch off for one hour. Recharge.**
- ☐ **No screens in the bedroom.**
- ☐ **Task-batch to reduce mental blocks and save time.**

DAY 27

Alter Your Brainwaves

> "Check on yourself as much as you check on your Instagram."
> – Unknown

On my path towards kicking my scrolling habit, I have become increasingly interested in the way tech can help us to be more relaxed, focused, and mindful around screens. It is increasingly possible to scroll less, and relax while *still using screens*, by using apps and devices that can actually help us to recharge.

I've tried out a great deal of tech innovation on this journey, and some of it is really quite impressive at helping me to feel more fulfilled and present. I present the best of it here. (Trust me, there was plenty that didn't make the cut.)

QUICK BRAINWAVE EXPLAINER

The five most commonly studied human brainwave forms are: Delta (0.5 to 4Hz); Theta (4 to 7Hz); Alpha (8 to 12Hz); Beta (13 to 30Hz); and Gamma (30 to 80Hz) (1). They all move at different speeds. These fluctuate within our brain throughout the day, depending on what we are doing.

Change your brainwave state and your brain will literally work at an altered pace.

Much of the best tech works by altering our brainwaves. These waves are measured by frequency. That is cycles per second, or hertz (Hz); they range from very slow to very fast.

Beta brainwaves

Beta brainwaves go fast – between about 12 and 35 Hz. Our brains tend not to relax when we are engaged in high-beta-level brainwave activity.

Um, like scrolling.

Think emails, Facebook, WhatsApp, any social media, news sites and so on.

Beta means the wide awake zone – in which you are focused and "on it". However, we only have a certain amount of that energy in the bank. That's why we sometimes feel so frazzled after a lengthy tech session.

We end up stressed, and accept it as the norm. Linda Stone called it "continuous partial attention", and said its shadow side is "over-stimulation and lack of fulfillment."

Alpha brainwaves

What is helpful for many people is less beta and more of the other brainwave states like "alpha" brainwaves. These measure between 8 and 12 Hz. At that frequency you are probably feeling relatively calm and relaxed.

Changing state is a core NLP concept and today we are aiming for less beta and more alpha.

> ➤ Swap out your screen kryptonite, (ie: doomscrolling, gaming, TikTok, emails), for one of the brainwave-altering

solutions below. Even if you switch for just 10 minutes, you may feel surprisingly refreshed and recharged.

It probably goes without saying, but do not use any of these apps or devices while driving or operating machinery.

Tech to change brainwave states

Othership

This breathing app helps you regulate your emotions and nervous system through guided breathwork. It's like a breathing disco: from beta to alpha in a few moments. You'll just have to try it. ($)

Binaural beats

Binaural beats apps, which play odd sounds at different frequencies, are proven to induce altered states of consciousness and to "modulate mood states" (2). That might mean less beta brainwaves (high stimulation) and more alpha waves (reducing stress and anxiety – a proper chill-out zone). I recommend an app called Binaural. You can actually choose any brainwaves with binaural beats – not just alpha. Professor Andrew Huberman recommends gamma waves at 40Hz for problem solving and focus, and that's what I'm listening to as I write this. ($)

Sensate

Sensate is a cool, pebble-shaped device that you place on your chest. It sends vibrations through your chest up into your head. It sounds odd, but it is very relaxing. It uses the natural power of sonic resonance to calm your body's nervous system, providing immediate relief and long-term benefits from regular use. If you use this, you'll have less of that beta-level stress. ($$)

Muse

This brain sensing headband is a personal meditation assistant that will gently guide you to a calm mind. Put on the Muse headband and earbuds, start the app, and close your eyes. You'll hear changing sounds of weather based on the real-time state of your brain. This can allow you to obtain a deeper sense of focus and motivation. This kind of enjoyable, in-depth exploration of brainwave states and EEG has been proven to improve mood states (3). ($$$)

(guide: $ = cheap with free options, $$ = mid-level tech relief, $$$ = expensive investment)

TO-DO LIST

- ☐ **Switch off for one hour. Recharge.**
- ☐ **No screens in the bedroom.**
- ☐ **Alter brainwave states with cutting edge apps and devices.**
- ☐ **Try deep alpha for relaxation and gamma for high-level focus on screens.**

DAY 28

Upgrade or Downgrade?

> *"We live in a cult of the upgrade right now. There's always something around the corner that will make whatever you think is cool right now feel obsolete."*
> – Colin Trevorrow

Is it possible to own a phone that doesn't turn us into a screen zombie? Every two years, I get a message from my phone provider. You probably do too. It asks if I'd like to "upgrade my device," and displays lots of shiny pictures of the latest phone which I just have to have.

It's hard to resist. I upgrade. But when I get the new device, I quickly acclimatize to the new normal and forget all its supposed perks.

Here are some "pro-level" and fairly radical solutions that, as a soon-to-be-graduate of this *30 Day Expert* program, you may want to consider. They are not for the faint-hearted. They are device upgrades/downgrades that will help you live life without the constant interruptions you've come to love – social media, maps, apps and so on. Let's look at them.

1. **The Light Phone** is a premium, minimal phone. It doesn't have social media, news, email, or internet. It's just a phone, it calls and texts. There is a headphone jack, bluetooth, and it can be used as a personal hotspot. It looks pretty – a bit like a tiny Kindle.
2. **Mudita Pure Phone.** Another modern minimalist phone. An eye-friendly E Ink display, high quality components,

with essentials only. Privacy is front and center, as is ultra-low EMFs.
3. **Gabb Phone.** This is a hugely popular phone for kids, which comes with no social media, no internet, and no games – and it works for adults too. There's a calculator, calendar, camera, clock, contact book, file manager, FM radio, music player, video player, and voice recorder. And that's it, although there is the ability to add more apps with parental consent. **Pinwheel** and **Troomi** are competitors which allow parents to customize their child's online experience.
4. **An old fashioned burner phone.** A "burner phone" is a cheap, prepaid mobile phone that you can destroy or discard when you no longer need it. But you're going to keep it. You'll be saving money, time, and attention, as well as spending less time scrolling. Old Nokias do the job particularly well, and have better battery life than an iPhone too.

IS THIS THE SOLUTION TO SOCIAL ADDICTION?

What do you use your device for? A study of 200 young adults found that most people use the internet to *"get involved in activities of social networks and online gaming"*. Factors which steered the participants to internet use included *"gaining random instant popularity on social media platforms... Users derive great satisfaction from Internet use and perceive it as a way of making up for their shortcomings, which, however, turns into a dependent relationship."* (1)

If this sounds like you, it may be worth considering one of these radical device solutions. You'll be able to check your messages, but there'll be no gaming, scrolling or likes.

> Attention is a finite resource. It has a limit. That's why so much of this program has been based around safeguarding our attention as much as possible. And if you upgrade/downgrade with one of these devices, you will have taken stopping scrolling to the next level.

So do you dare to go minimal?

TO-DO LIST

- ☐ **Switch off for one hour. Recharge.**
- ☐ **No screens in the bedroom.**
- ☐ **Consider minimalist devices for the ultimate no-scroll life.**

DAY 29

Nuance

> *"Technology can be our best friend, and technology can also be the biggest party pooper of our lives. It interrupts our own story, interrupts our ability to have a thought or a daydream, to imagine something wonderful, because we're too busy bridging the walk from the cafeteria back to the office on the cell phone."*
>
> – Steven Spielberg

We are at the victory lap stage of your *30 Day Expert* program. Today we continue to think about the future. You may prefer to introduce a more nuanced approach as you reach expert status around screens. Here's why.

For many people (like me) the problem isn't actually the presence of screens in the house, but the connected nature of those screens. It's the internet, 5G and Wi-Fi. It's the sheer addictiveness of being connected to people through the internet. It's not television on its own, or an e-reader.

This provides a high level of addiction and that is what seems to be so hard to give up.

Let me give you an example. If I'm reading a book on my Kindle for three hours with no distractions, I consider that to be recharging. I can think deeply and cultivate focus.

If I'm reading the Kindle app on my phone *while* receiving notifications from WhatsApp, Instagram, TikTok, email, Facebook, Messenger and more, I'm clearly not thinking deeply. I'm obviously not cultivating focus. I'm obviously mindlessly scrolling. I'm not present. I'm not recharging. And personally, I know I'm not living my best life, although I am maintaining seven different WhatsApp chats.

EYES UP!

Here's a fun screen-related exercise for more energy. Professor Andrew Huberman says the simple act of looking upwards creates a wakefulness signal to the brain. This is down to the scientifically-proven connection between brain stem circuits and other neural circuits that control wakefulness.

He recommends raising your eyes and holding that gaze for 15 seconds. Other ways to plug into this research are to hold your device higher when using it, and place your computer screen at eye level or higher in your WFH office space.

Oh, and he does acknowledge how laughably simple this sounds (1).

So, we have started with a total screen ban, which is important for clarity and a reset. But we can hone it once you officially become a 30 Day Expert.

Just remember, if your discipline starts to slip, you'll have to get strict again.

- ➢ Fill out your post-program screen schedule below. Will it be a hardline no-screens policy? Or as discussed above, will there be some exceptions?

My post program screen schedule:

_____

_____

_____

_____

Example: I continue to switch off for one hour a day and recharge. But during that time I'll allow myself to read my Kindle or watch films (with no other scrolling) as these things help me relax and make me happy.

TO-DO LIST

- ☐ **Switch off for one hour. Recharge.**
- ☐ **No screens in the bedroom.**
- ☐ **Write your more nuanced future screen use plan.**

DAY 30

1170 Reasons To Celebrate

> "When you stop and look around, this life is pretty amazing."
>
> – Dr. Seuss

It was New Year's Day, and I was walking down the street in West London. In front of me, there was a crisp, beautiful winter sunset, the sky aflame on the first day of the year. I fought the urge to reach for my phone. My hand hovered above my pocket, desperate to pull out my shiny device of delights. (I still maintain that that sunset would have made a wonderful Instagram photo. Especially if I'd used the Lo-Fi filter, goddammit. And I could have emailed it to my friends too. Or tweeted it. Or even put it on LinkedIn. No, that would be a step too far. Who looks at LinkedIn?)

This was many years ago, but the idea for this *30 Day Expert* program was born then. I knew that I needed to be creating more time in my life. I wanted to live without so much distraction.

That's what you've done over the last month too. You've cut down on that distraction. You've committed to change. And now it's time for a little self-congratulation.

Here is the extra time you have created in your life over the last 30 days.

- Week 1: You created 105 extra scroll-free minutes
- Week 2: You created 210 extra scroll-free minutes

- Week 3: You created 315 extra scroll-free minutes
- Week 4 (plus days 29 and 30) You created 540 extra scroll-free minutes

Total: 1170 minutes (19 and a half hours)

This is a considerable amount of extra time in your life. Now consider what would happen if you kept this going for a year.

> Ask yourself what you can achieve with this frankly crazy amount of extra time. At this rate, you'll create almost 30 full working days (or six working weeks) of extra time per year. Commit to continuing on your healthy screen time journey for all this space in your life.

You've done so much right over the past 30 days. You've reached expert scroller status. You've learnt the behavioral science, the NLP and the biohacks. You're now scrolling healthier, and you didn't have to throw your phone away.

Now keep it going. Maintain that winning streak. Keep using your accountability buddy. Keep escaping the screens. Keep recharging. And keep noticing how much better, calmer, and more present you seem to be.

Back to that sunset on New Year's Day. I decided to take radical action to create more space. I put my TV presenting commitments in the UK on hold, left the keys to my apartment with a friend, and boarded a plane to as far away as possible. 24 hours later, I groggily arrived in Sydney to finish my third book.

"It's not a holiday", I protested almost daily, to anybody who'd listen. But, okay, it was close to it.

I tasted fine wine in the Hunter Valley, and cheap BBQ'd bangers by the beach. I went to gigs at the Olympic Stadium and the

Sydney Opera House. I made lifelong friends in coffee shops. I swam in the sea most mornings (and learnt not to get caught in rip tides). I took hour-long bus journeys (and the view was so good I didn't check my iPhone once). I visited my local pie shop at least four times a week. I woke up to the sound of waves and a view of the sea.

I spent lots of time with my best mate and his wife, and watched their baby daughter grow day-by-day. I saw England win the Ashes (a cricket reference that most Americans won't get, but this was a big deal… for me anyway.) I was out-drunk by a 75-year old. I walked across hot coals. I spent way more than I earnt. Oh yeah, and I wrote a book.

But what did I actually learn from my holiday trip to Sydney?

What those three months gave me was something I never normally have enough of: time.

I had the time to work out in the gym every day. The time to wait at the bus stop for half an hour and not care. The time to walk along the beach, just because I can. Even the time to ponder why Aussie pies are so very tasty.

Most of all, I had the time to think.

As the Roman philosopher Seneca said.

"Time discovers truth."

This is really a book about time, and creating more of it for the things you love. I have been learning, studying and teaching Neuro-Linguistic Programming for around two decades now, while working full-time in TV, and this issue of focus, distraction, loss of time and screens has preoccupied me more than any other.

I was so obsessed with finding the answer, that I took it to extremes. I flew to Australia in order to step off the hamster wheel of two jobs, a hectic party and social life and not enough time and space for reflection, but I actually didn't need to go that far to achieve the same thing.

When I created more time in my life, I had the space to think about what was important to me: the work I care about; the people I love; my purpose; what I want to do next; the projects I want to work on; the things I want to learn; the places I want to see; and the people I want to see them with.

And I could have just as easily done that at home. I returned from that trip 10 years ago this year, and I'm happy to say that, by not working as hard, by not scrolling so much (yes, iPhones were almost as distracting 10 years ago as they are now!), and by switching off and recharging, I can now create that space for reflection and truth whenever I need. Sure, I may not be sipping on a chilled glass of something nice in the Hunter Valley at the same time, but the extra headspace is what counts

> Next time you ditch the scroll to create three more minutes (or three hours, or three days, or three months), what you are creating is time. So what truth will you discover with that extra time?

TO-DO LIST

- [ ] **Switch off for one hour. Recharge.**
- [ ] **No screens in the bedroom.**
- [ ] **Congratulate yourself on becoming a 30 Day Expert.**
- [ ] **Keep going - you'll create *six working weeks* of extra time per year.**

DAY 31 ONWARDS

Day 31 Onwards – Regular Refreshers

"I cannot preserve my health and spirits unless I spend four hours a day at least – and it is commonly more than that – sauntering through the woods and over the hills and fields absolutely free from all worldly engagements."

– Henry David Thoreau

Well here we are. You've completed the program. You've applied yourself and learnt new skills. But personally, I find the work is never *quite* done. Just when I think I've got my scroll game sorted, I'll catch myself trying to do six different things at once and not really focusing on any of them. So I encourage you to: a) continue along the road that you've stuck to for the last 30 days; . And b) come back here intermittently in the future for a little refresher.

So by returning to a number of these techniques again I give myself periodic reminders on my scrolling boundaries, which really helps.

- ➢ If you've enjoyed applying the skills of Neuro-Linguistic Programming and becoming a 30 Day Expert, why not check out my other books and follow another month-long program. You could even Learn NLP with me.

If you enjoyed this book and have found you spend a bit less time on screens, I'd be very grateful for a review so I can spread the word. Finally, keep that healthy scrolling going, and notice how much extra time you have.

And now, a sneak preview of another 30 Day Expert program you might like...

LEARN NLP

Learn NLP: Master Neuro-Linguistic Programming (the Non-Boring Way) in 30 Days

Here is one question I get asked a lot.

Er, what exactly is NLP?

Neuro-Linguistic Programming (NLP) helps us improve the way we communicate with ourselves and other people. It studies "what works." It is a wildly popular set of skills and theories first developed in the 1970s, and perhaps "neuro-hacking" would be a better name. Here's why it's worth studying in this *30 Day Expert* program.

- NLP studies how people do things well.
- NLP is a set of skills that improves your communication.
- NLP helps you manage your moods and run your own life more successfully.
- NLP can help with your personal development and the development of others.
- NLP is used a lot in business, self-improvement, sport, sales, therapy and coaching.

When I first started learning NLP many years ago, I was working as a radio presenter in Manchester, UK. My teacher impressed on me the importance of practicing these skills as much as possible "in the real world" to get feedback and to improve. He said what was important was to be proficient at using NLP, not just having a piece of paper proclaiming that I was a practitioner.

Good point. A certificate looks nice but isn't very helpful out in the world. So I came up with a plan. I would use the linguistic part of NLP to try to make my radio show better. In addition, every radio show wants more listeners. So I would try to encourage new people to listen and for longer too.

For months I used my show as a training ground. It's important to emphasize that I didn't always get it right. In truth, I wasn't very good at this NLP malarkey but there I was engaging with it and trying to pick it up day after day.

There was one particular afternoon when I felt that I'd been particularly unsubtle. I had been trying out a new skill that I had learned on my course. And, um, it hadn't quite gone to plan. Obviously the only way to improve is to make mistakes and learn from them, but I think on that particular day I just sounded a bit weird.

After I came off air, my boss called me into his office. He sat back and put hands behind his head. I gulped. I was desperately trying to remember the body language element of what I've learned on my NLP course. Were hands behind the head a good thing or not?

"I don't know what you've done", he said, "but your listening figures have gone through the roof."

At that station, I presented the DriveTime show. In fact my listening figures had gone up so much that they had overtaken the Breakfast Show. That is something rare in the world of radio.

The reason for telling this story is not a humble brag, honest. Okay, maybe a tiny bit. But my NLP teacher told me to "practice, practice

practice" and that is what I did. Not only did it help me actually learn, it turned out the skills worked rather well.

Was this because of the NLP techniques? Possibly or possibly not. The Breakfast Show presenter was brilliant and it may have been luck, advertising or shifting listening habits. But I like to think Neuro-Linguistic Programming had something to do with it.

Over the next 30 days, I will encourage you to use the skills, get involved and embrace the hands-on approach that helped me.

Learn NLP is on sale now and remember to let me know how you get on over on my website, tonywrighton.com.

REFERENCES

What To Expect

1. https://www.ncbi.nlm.nih.gov/pmc/articles/PMC5574844/
2. https://pubmed.ncbi.nlm.nih.gov/20692047/
3. https://www.sciencedaily.com/releases/2020/09/200928191218.htm
4. https://www.cnbc.com/2019/09/22/heres-how-many-hours-american-workers-spend-on-email-each-day.html
5. https://influencermarketinghub.com/tiktok-stats/

Day 1

1. https://www.researchgate.net/publication/351048905_Screen_time_and_its_impact_on_health
2. https://www.frontiersin.org/articles/10.3389/fpubh.2021.794307/full
3. https://pubmed.ncbi.nlm.nih.gov/26239965/
4. https://www.statisticbrain.com/new-years-resolution-statistics/
5. https://www.gsb.stanford.edu/sites/default/files/publication-pdf/step_by_step_obhdp_for_web.pdf

Day 3

1. https://hbr.org/2015/01/why-a-messy-workspace-undermines-your-persistence

Day 4

1. https://www.cell.com/current-biology/comments/S0960-9822(13)00764-1

Day 5

1. https://www.theguardian.com/technology/2018/jul/14/mobile-phones-cancer-inconvenient-truths

Day 6

1. https://www.ncbi.nlm.nih.gov/pmc/articles/PMC8438907/
2. https://journals.sagepub.com/doi/10.1177/0956797614524581
3. https://scholar.dominican.edu/cgi/viewcontent.cgi?article=1265&context=news-releases

Day 7

1. https://www.statisticbrain.com/new-years-resolution-statistics/
2. https://pubmed.ncbi.nlm.nih.gov/20483853/

Day 8

1. https://www.ncbi.nlm.nih.gov/pmc/articles/PMC7320888/
2. https://www.ncbi.nlm.nih.gov/pmc/articles/PMC7320888/
3. https://journals.physiology.org/doi/full/10.1152/japplphysiol.01413.2009
4. https://academic.oup.com/sleep/article-abstract/43/Supplement_1/A12/5847498?redirectedFrom=fulltext

Day 9

1. https://www.ncbi.nlm.nih.gov/pmc/articles/PMC2582340/
2. https://www.ncbi.nlm.nih.gov/pmc/articles/PMC2582340/

Day 10

1. https://link.springer.com/article/10.1007/s40123-022-00540-9
2. https://www.aao.org/eye-health/tips-prevention/computer-usage
3. https://link.springer.com/article/10.1007/s40123-022-00540-9

Day 12

1. https://www.ncbi.nlm.nih.gov/pmc/articles/PMC5556586/
2. https://www.sciencedaily.com/releases/2020/09/200928191218.htm
3. https://bmjopen.bmj.com/content/9/1/e023191

Day 13

1. https://link.springer.com/article/10.1007/s12144-021-02020-y

Day 14

1. https://iaap-journals.onlinelibrary.wiley.com/doi/full/10.1111/aphw.12302
2. https://psycnet.apa.org/record/2013-35881-026
3. https://www.ncbi.nlm.nih.gov/pmc/articles/PMC9291624/
4. https://ggia.berkeley.edu/practice/how_would_you_treat_a_friend?_ga=2.224147739.1811588886.1665392130-1540413946.1665152650

Day 15

1. https://www.afcpe.org/news-and-publications/the-standard/2018-3/the-power-of-accountability/

Day 16

1. https://www.dominican.edu/sites/default/files/2020-02/gailmatthews-harvard-goals-researchsummary.pdf
2. https://tim.blog/2014/07/14/autoresponse/

Day 17

1. https://www.ncbi.nlm.nih.gov/pmc/articles/PMC7674395/
2. https://pubmed.ncbi.nlm.nih.gov/20307805/
3. https://edition.cnn.com/2012/09/20/health/mobile-society-neck-pain/

Day 18

1. https://lifehacker.com/science-explains-why-our-best-ideas-come-in-the-shower-5987858
2. http://archive.boston.com/lifestyle/health/articles/2012/02/27/when_being_distracted_is_a_good_thing/

Day 20

1. https://journals.physiology.org/doi/full/10.1152/jn.01042.2014#B8

Day 21

1. https://www.researchgate.net/publication/345650647_A_Link_Between_Colors_and_Emotions_A_Study_of_Undergraduate_Females
2. https://www.ncbi.nlm.nih.gov/pmc/articles/PMC5813944/

Day 23

1. https://www.nytimes.com/2016/01/22/opinion/the-eight-second-attention-span.html?_r=3
2. https://www.crossrivertherapy.com/average-human-attention-span
3. https://pubmed.ncbi.nlm.nih.gov/26121498/
4. https://www.sciencedirect.com/science/article/abs/pii/S0747563212000799

Day 26

1. https://news.virginia.edu/content/study-smartphone-alerts-increase-inattention-and-hyperactivity
2. https://www.apa.org/topics/research/multitasking

Day 27

1. https://www.ncbi.nlm.nih.gov/books/NBK539805/
2. https://www.ncbi.nlm.nih.gov/pmc/articles/PMC4428073/
3. https://sources.mandala.library.virginia.edu/source/eeg-neurofeedback-optimising-performance-i-review-cognitive-and-affective-outcome-healthy

Day 28

1. https://www.ncbi.nlm.nih.gov/pmc/articles/PMC6198588/

Day 29

1. https://hubermanlab.com/the-science-of-vision-eye-health-and-seeing-better/

Printed in Poland
by Amazon Fulfillment
Poland Sp. z o.o., Wrocław